LARVA LEGIS AQUILIAE

For Robert Feenstra
as a token of our esteem and affecti~
5 October 2000

D1425564

Christianus Thomasius
Potentissimi Borussiæ Regis Consiliarius Intimus,
Universitatis Fridericianæ Director. Professor
Primar. et Facultatis Juridicæ Ordinarius etc
Natus Lips. d. 1 Jan. 1655. Denatus Hala d. 23. Sept. 1728.

LARVA LEGIS AQUILIAE

THE MASK OF THE *LEX AQUILIA* TORN OFF THE ACTION FOR DAMAGE DONE.

A legal treatise
by
CHRISTIAN THOMASIUS (1655–1728)

Edited and translated from the Latin by
MARGARET HEWETT
(University of Cape Town)

With an essay
'Christian Thomasius, the Reception of Roman Law
and the History of the *Lex Aquilia*'
by
REINHARD ZIMMERMANN
(University of Regensburg)

HART PUBLISHING
Oxford • Portland, Oregon
2000

Hart Publishing
Oxford and Portland, Oregon

Published in North America (US and Canada) by
Hart Publishing
c/o International Specialized Book Services
5804 NE Hassalo Street
Portland, Oregon
97213-3644
USA

Distributed in Netherlands, Belgium and Luxembourg by
Intersentia, Churchillaan 108
B2900 Schoten
Antwerpen
Belgium

Hart Publishing is a specialist legal publisher based in Oxford, England.
To order further copies of this book or to request a list of other publications
please write to:

Hart Publishing, Salters Boatyard, Folly Bridge,
Abingdon Rd, Oxford, OX1 4LB
Telephone: +44 (0)1865 245533 Fax: +44 (0) 1865 794882
email: mail@hartpub.co.uk
WEBSITE: http//:www.hartpub.co.uk

British Library Cataloguing in Publication Data
Data Available

ISBN 1-84113-223-3 (paperback)

Typeset by John Saunders, Typeset and Design, Reading
Printed and bound in Great Britain by
Lightning Source UK Ltd

PREFACE

his translation of Christian Thomasius' *Larva Legis Aquiliae* had its beginnings many
ars ago in the lecture rooms of the University of Cape Town. Both Professor
immermann and I found the text a useful and important source for our teaching of
e law, but we considered that Thomasius' thoughts deserved a wider audience, and
r that a translation was perhaps desirable. The *Larva* is significant not only for legal
storians but, as Professor Zimmermann says in his essay, 'there are also a number of
issages which should still appeal to modern lawyers interested in the doctrinal
undations of the law of delict.' Pressure of work prevented our completing this
oklet earlier, but the beginning of the new Millenium seemed an appropriate
casion finally to launch it.

It is necessary to draw attention to the fact that although this dissertation was
fended by the doctorial respondent, Gaius Matthias Arend, on 28 April 1703, we
cided not to use the *editio prima,* or the editions of 1730, 1743 or 1774, but the
750 edition which appeared best suited for the purposes of reproduction. For
terest's sake, however, we have included the title page of the 1703 edition, which
ves the name of the respondent and the date of the disputation. The 1730 reprint
kewise includes the name of the respondent, merely stating *recusa 1730.* The 1743
lition, however, makes a substantial addition in the form of a German translation of
e title of the treatise. It is only in the 1750 edition that Arend's name is omitted, as
is in the 1774 edition. The 1750 edition was probably a reprint of a series of disser-
tions all by Thomasius. Certainly, the 1774 edition was one of such a series,
printed in four volumes, 1773 – 1780.

For information and a chance to inspect the various editions, I must express my
preciation to the Library staff of the Max-Planck-Institut für Europäische
echtsgeschichte, Frankfurt, to David Ferris and Mary L Person of the Langdell Hall
aw Library at Harvard, and to Prof Laurent Mayali and the staff of the Robbins
ollection, University of California at Berkeley. Needless to say, the support and
onsideration I have received in all matters from Ms L Omar and the staff of our
CT Library is as always the *sine qua non* of research such as this in Cape Town.

Furthermore, my appreciation and thanks for their help and interest go to Mr Olaf
ichter of Waiblingen who provided me with a copy of the Catalogue of Thomasius'
brary and a biographical note. Without doubt this manuscript would never have seen
e light of day without the original typing assistance of Mrs Carin Tobias of Cape

Town, and likewise I owe a debt both for critical comment and proficiency on the
to Miss Helen Scott, my research assistant at UCT.

Last and most important, both Reinhard Zimmermann and I would like
dedicate this slim volume to Professor Mr Robert Feenstra. Not only has he give
the benefit of his vast expertise on the *Larva*, but he has been for many yea
constant source of support and inspiration. This is a token of our esteem and affect

Margaret Hewett

CONTENTS

BIBLIOGRAPHICAL NOTE

editing and translating a text of this nature, it is desirable to pay considerable atten-
n to the sources used by the writer, and to provide a bibliographical listing (p xi
ow) and bibliographical notes.

A noteworthy feature of this short dissertation is that of the approximately 30 texts
ntioned, only 9 are cited directly. The remainder are citations within citations. It is
ar that Schilter[1] and Stryk are the main supports on which Thomasius bases his
uments, and they in turn support their arguments with batteries of citations. In
nposing the Bibliography I have listed all citations but marked direct citations with
in the left hand margin.

It is my policy to try to identify and verify each citation, and where possible in a
atemporary edition. In the Bibliography the editions examined physically have been
icated by *. In some cases more than one edition of the same text has been
mined.

In addition I have a microfilm of the catalogue of Thomasius' books, offered for sale
his widow in 1739. The title page of the catalogue states that the BIBLIOTHECA
IOMASIANA containing books and pamphlets on a wide range of subjects in
tin and German, but also in French, Italian, Spanish and English would be offered
sale by public auction in Halle from 10:00–12:00 am and from 2:00–4:00 pm on
: 6 July 1739 and on the days following. The auction would take place at the
omasius residence.

The catalogue, running to 496 pages, lists many thousands of works. In most
tances it provides brief information regarding date, place of publication and
ding. Pamphlets are often grouped together, as are certain major works. There is no
parent reason, for instance, why Matthaeus' *De iure gladii* should have been sold
lividually but his *De criminibus* lumped together with Wissenbach's *Disputationes ad*
tituta and also Matthaeus' *De auctionibus* (1653), which incidentally is inaccurately
ed as *De actionibus*. The catalogue is divided firstly by topic and then within each
ic by format. Thus under *Libri Juridici, Canonici et Morales* there are 187 entries in
io, 449 in quarto, 277 in octavo and 71 in duodecimo. Very few are duplicates. In
lition there are 3273 disputations on a variety of subjects, including Law. These
putations seem to have been classified very generally. The listing is headed
sputationes Theologicae, Iuridicae, Historicae, Philosophicae, Miscellaneae nec non

---

[1] Thomasius wrote the preface to the third edition of Schilter's *Praxis Juris Romani.*

rariores alphabetico autorum ordine collectae. Thus several works by the same author a
collected together, eg 17 under Schacher, 8 under Schilterus, 17 under Schöpfer.
the last case six of the seven are patently legal works but one wonders about *
Pulmone Infantis natante.* Thomasius' score is 120 – certainly one of the highest. H(
these were sold is not clear. Presumably not individually.

For the purposes of this publication it has not been possible or desirable to loca
and verify every citation in the edition listed in Thomasius' library catalogu
especially considering the majority are second-hand citations, but for interest's sa
the edition listed in the catalogue has been entered in the Bibliography and marked
(This includes the citations within citations.) But as no serious bibliographi(
research has been devoted to this catalogue, and as even a casual glance indicat
inaccuracies, no great significance must be attached to comments relating to it.

Such auctioneer's catalogues can be extremely useful but they also have limitatior
First, the compilers of the catalogues are often inaccurate in recording titles, dates
editions etc. Also the fact that a text does not appear in the catalogue is no proof th
the owner did not in fact possess the text, especially where, as here, the books we
auctioned 10 years after Thomasius' death.

It is interesting to note, however, that considering the wide range of text, presun
ably available to Thomasius at the time of writing the *Larva,* he chose to restrict k
citations. On this see also Prof. Zimmerman's essay p. 68.

BIBLIOGRAPHY OF
WORKS CITED IN THE TEXT

ιe abbreviated form of citation as used in the English text appears in the first column; in the
:ond the name or names by which the author was generally known and an extended title of
e book.

The reader is reminded that many of the texts cited appear as part of a longer citation. See
bliographical Note p ix. Primary citations are indicated by the # in the left-hand margin.

An * after the date of an edition indicates that the citation in the text has been checked in
e edition thus marked. The dates of editions as given are not all inclusive. An † after the date
an edition indicates that the text thus marked appears in the catalogue of Thomasius' books.

BOECKELMANN, *Differentiae juris civilis et canonici*	Johannes Fridericus Boeckelmann, *Tractatus postumus de differentiis juris civilis et canonici et hodierni* (Utrecht, 1694, 1697, 1721,1737*)
BRUNNEMANN, *Ad Pandectas*	Johannes Brunnemannus, *Commentarius in quinquaginta libros Pandectarum ... opus theoretico-practicum* (Frankfurt, 1670†; 1692*; 1762*)
CARPZOVIUS, *Jurisprudentia forensis*	Benedictus Carpzovius, *Jurisprudentia forensis Romano-Saxonica secundum ordinem constitutionum D. Augusti electoris Saxoniae.* Also known as *Definitiones forenses* (Frankfurt, 1650*; Leipzig, 1668; 1684†)
COVARRUVIAS, *Variae resolutiones*	Didacus Covarruvias (Covarrubias a Leyva), *Variae resolutiones* in *Opera Omnia* (Lyons, 1584*)
ENGELBRECHT	Georg Engelbrecht, *Compendium iurisprudentiae ex genuinis iuris naturae, ethices ac politices principiis, Pandectarum, Codicis, Novellarum, iuris canonici, recessum imperii constitutionum...textibus secundum ordinem Digestorum concinnatum...* (Helmstedt, 1637)
J FABER, *Ad Inst.*	Johannes Faber, *Commentarii in quatuor Institutionum libros* (numerous editions after 1488; Leiden, 1557*)

GIESEBERT, *Justinianus Harmonicus*   Henricus Giesebert (Gisebert), *Justinianus Harmonicus exhibens introductionem ad iuris prudentiam hodiernam communem* (Lübeck, 166? 1670†)

GOLDAST, *Reichs-Satzung*   Melchior Hamenveltus Goldast (von Hamensfeld), *Reichs-Satzung des H.R.R. Kayser* etc. (Hanover, 1609)

GROENEWEGEN, *De legibus abrogatis* Simon van Groenewegen van der Made, *Tracta de legibus abrogatis et inusitatis in Hollandia vicin isque regionibus* (Leiden, 1649*; Nijmegen, 1664 Amsterdam, 1669*†)

\# KULPIS   Johannes George von Kulpis (Culpisius), *Diatr historico juridica de receptione juris Romani* (origi- nally published under the pseudonym Conradus Sincerus, Leipzig 1682; 1713†)

\# MEVIUS, *Decisiones*   David Mevius, *Decisiones super causis praecipuis a summum tribunal regium Wismariense delatis* (Wismar 1657; Frankfurt, 1712*†)

MATTHAEUS, *De criminibus*   Antonius Matthaeus II, *De criminibus ad lib. 47 48 Digesti commentarius. Adjecta est brevis iuris municipalis interpretatio* (Utrecht, 1644*; Amsterdam, 1661*†; Antwerp, 1761*)

\# OLDENDORP, *Actiones forenses*   Johannes Oldendorp (Oldendorf), *Actionum forensium progymnasmata* (Erfurt, 1608†). Checked in *Opera* (Aalen, reprint 1966* of Base edition of 1559)

OOSTERGA
(See REGNERI)

PAPONIUS, *Decisiones*   Jean Papon, *Recueil d'arrests notable des cours souveraines de France* (Lyons, 1559*; Geneva, 1648*)

PISTORIS, *Quaestiones*   Hartmann Pistoris, *Quaestionum iuris tam Roma quam Saxonici liber primus* (Leipzig, 1579 - 158? Jena, 1597-1609†)

PRAESES,*Dissertatio*
(See THOMASIUS)

REGNERI, *Censura Belgica*

Cyprianus Regneri ab Oosterga, *Censura Belgica seu novae notae et animadversiones in libros IV Institutionum* (Utrecht, 1648†, 1661*†)

RICHTER, *Decisiones juris*

Christoph Philipp Richter, *Centuria variarum juris decisionum, quam plurimos casus illustres, singulares et valde utiles diversasque materias judiciorum, contractuum, ultimarum voluntatum, delictorum et plures alias continentium in duas partes divisa* (Jena, 1663*)

ROSBACH, *Comparatio juris*

Johannes Emmerich von Rosbach, *De comparatione juris civilis et canonici* (Strasbourg, 1616*) also bound behind Rittershusius, *Differentiae juris civilis et canonici* (Strasbourg, 1638*)

SCHACHER, *Collegium practicum*

Quirinus Schacher, *Collegium practicum iuxta titulos Pandectas, iuris civilis continuo serie connexos, conceptum usitatissimis actionum et exceptionum formulis instructum* (Leipzig, 1678)

SCHILTER, *Exercitationes ad ndectas e Praxis juris Romani)*

Johannes Schilter, *Exercitationes ad quinquaginta libros Digestorum* (Jena, 1675-1680). A new edition was published in Jena in 1698 with the title *Praxis iuris Romani*. See below.

SCHILTER, *Praxis juris Romani*

Johannes Schilter, *Praxis juris Romani in foro Germanico, iuxta ordinem edicti perpetui et Pandectarum Justiniani* (Jena, 1698†; Frankfurt and Leipzig, 1713*). The 1713 edition contains a preface by Thomasius.

SCHOEPFERUS, *Synopsis juris privati*

Johannes Joachim Schoepferus, *Synopsis juris privati Romani et forensis* (1595†; Frankfurt/Oder, 1702*)

SCHNEIDEWINUS, *Ad Inst.*

Johannes Schneidewinus (Schneidewein), *In quattuor Institutionum imperialium Justiniani libros commentarii* (Strasbourg, 1595*; Venice, 1701*; Cologne, 1724*)

SCHWENDENDÖRFF, *Ad Ekoltum* — Bartholomeus Leonhardus Schwendendörff (Svendendörff, Swendendörff), Notes on Amadeus Eckolt, *Compendiosa Pandectarum tractatio* (Leipzig, 1680†, 1694)

SCHWENDENDÖRFFERUS, *De actionibus forensibus* — Bartholomeus Leonhardus Schwendendörffer *Expositio actionum forensium* (?) (Leipzig, 167·

SICHARDUS, *Ad C.* — Johannes Sichardus, *Commentarius in Codicem* (Frankfurt, 1565, 1586, 1598, 1595†)

STRUVIUS, *Syntagma iurisprudentia* — Gustavus Adolphus Struvius, *Syntagma iurispr dentiae secundum ordinem Pandectarum concin-natum* (1658-1663; Jena, 1702*)

\# STRYK, *De actionibus* — Samuel Stryk, *Tractatus de actionibus forensibus investigandis et caute eligendis* (Halle, 1696; als Opera Omnia, Frankfurt/Leipzig, 1743-1755)

\# STRYK, *Usus Modernus Pandectarum* — Samuel Stryk (Frankfurt, 1690†,1743-1752*; Florence, 1837-1891*)

THOMAE, *De noxia animalium* — Johannes Thomae, *Tractatus de noxia animaliu* (Jena and Leipzig, 1653†; Frankfurt, 1690)

\# THOMASIUS, *Dissertatio* — Christian Thomasius (*Praeses*, R. Chr. von Hal respondens), *Dissertatio de usu actionum poenaliu duplum et in quadruplum in foris Germaniae* (169

TREUTLER, *Disputationes* — Hieronymus Treutler, *Selectarum disputationur Jus Civile Justinianeum quinquaginta libris Pandectarum comprehensum* (Marburg, 1628*)

VAN LEEUWEN, *Censura forensis* — Simon van Leeuwen, *Censura forensis, theoretic practica, id est totius Juris Civilis Romani usuque recepti et practici methodica collatio* (Leyden, 16(Amsterdam, 1678, 1685*; Leyden, 1741*)

ZOBELIUS, *Differentiae juris* — Christoph Zobelius, *Differentiae iuris Civilis et Saxonici in quattuor partes distributae* (Leipzig, 1598*, 1610†)

THE MASK
OF THE
LEX AQUILIA

TORN OFF
THE ACTION FOR DAMAGE
DONE

AS RECEIVED
IN THE COURTS OF THE GERMANS

A LEGAL TREATISE

BY

CHRISTIAN THOMASIUS, JURIST

MEMBER OF THE PRIVY COUNCIL OF THE MOST
POWERFUL KING OF PRUSSIA

DIRECTOR OF THE ROYAL FREDERICK UNIVERSITY
PROFESSOR PRIMARIUS OF LAW AND DEAN OF THE LAW FACULTY

HALLE IN THE DUCHY OF MAGDEBURG
HENDEL PRESS, 1750

LARVA
LEGIS AQUILIÆ
DETRACTA
ACTIONI DE DAMNO DATO,
RECEPTÆ
IN FORIS GERMANORUM.

SUMMARIA.

Aqui-

THE MASK
OF THE *LEX AQUILIA*
TORN OFF
THE ACTION FOR DAMAGE
DONE
AS RECEIVED
IN THE COURTS OF THE GERMANY

SUMMARY

1. The status of the debate and the method of discussion
2. Nature dictates that damage done should be made good
3. Also damage done from mere negligence
4. Also damage done by accident
5. Generally, however, the owner bears the loss for accident
6. The concurrence of intent with intent or negligence with negligence with a view to the damage suffered by both parties
7. In a similar concurrence regarding accident, the loss falls on the owner
8. Therefore it must only be proved that the damage was done by the defendant, not how it was done
9. The damage done by a madman or an infant must be made good from their property
10. This action arises not from delict but from equity flowing from the nature of ownership.
11. Hence this action is granted only to the owner, even though there is no precise requirement to prove ownership
12. This action is purely reipersecutory
13. Also heirs are liable in terms thereof
14. In the case where several persons have done damage payment by one releases the rest
15. An apology as to why no authorities have been cited hitherto
16. Among the Romans, the *lex Aquilia* derogated all preceding laws

Aquiliæ. §. XVII. .... §. XVIII. .... dolum
& negligentiam minimam. §. XIX. L. Aquiliæ actionem locum
non habere, si damnum datum per .... negligentiam, quæ intuitu contractus non imputatur. §. XX. Dubium! an actio L.
Aquiliæ pœnalis sit, an rei persecutoria ... mixta. §. XXI. Rationes, quod sit pœnalis, sed .... sufficientes. §. XXII. Paulum habuisse actionem L. Aquiliæ pro rei persecutoria & Ulpiano contradixisse. §. XXIII. Actionem L. Aquiliæ tanquam pœnalem non dari contra heredes. §. XXIV. Plures si damnum dederint, unius solutione reliquos non liberari. §. XXV. Adversus furiosos & Infantes actionem legis Aquiliæ non dari. §. XXVI.
Nec meliorem hic rationem dari posse, quam quia pœnalis est.
§. XXVII. Comparatio furiosi cum quadrupede quatenus hic
procedat. §. XXVIII. Unde etiam dicitur ex delicto oriri.
§. XXIX. Actio Legis Aquiliæ datur adversus inficiantes in duplum. §. XXX. Jure Canonico damnum dans ultra veram damni restitutionem non tenetur can. fraternitas Cap. 12. quæst. 2.
§. XXXI. Eodem jure actio de damno dato datur contra heredes can. 3. Cap. 16. q. 6. §. XXXII. Et cap. ult. X. de Sepulturis.
§. XXXIII. Non tamen ultra vires hereditatis cap. 5. X. de raptoribus. §. XXXIV. Igitur Jure Canonico heredes tenentur
generaliter ad restitutionem damni per dolum defuncti dati.
§. XXXV. Et multo magis si damnum culpa defuncti datum sit.
§. XXXVI. Notatur Cl. Bœkelmannus. §. XXXVII. Leges an-
tiquæ Germanorum de restitutione damni dati non conveniunt
cum Lege Aquilia. §. XXXVIII. Capitula speculi Suevici de damnorum restitutione. §. XXXIX. Capitula Speculi Saxonici.
§. XL. Ostenditur actionem de damno dato reparando secundum utrumque speculum esse rei persecutoriam. §. XLI. Quamvis dissentiat Dn. Schilterus. §. XLII. Cui respondetur. §. XLIII.
Moribus Germaniæ hodiernis petitur saltem simplex damni æstimatio. §. XLIV. Unde actio legis Aquiliæ exulat, nisi in specie
sit recepta, ut Jure Borussico. §. XLV. Inconvenientia & con-
fusio

---

[1] Reading *parum* for *varum* as in the 1703 and 1774 editions

§. I.

Um larvam legis Aquiliæ detrahere volumus actioni de damno dato, qua hactenus Germani in foro usi sunt, non est animus exponere omnia, quæ ad naturam sive actionis legis Aquiliæ, sive actionis Germanorum de damno dato pertinent, sed reliquis omissis saltem ostendere, quod actio nostra, qua utimur, ab actione legis Aquiliæ magis differat, quam avis a quadrupe-

A 3 de,

§ I

WHILE I wish to strip the mask of the *lex Aquilia* from the action concerning damage done, which the Germans have hitherto used in court, it is not my intention to expound every detail which pertains to the nature either of the action under the *lex Aquilia* or of the German action for damage done, but leaving aside all else, I intend only to show that the action which we use is as different from the Aquilian action as a bird from a fourfooted beast,

de, etsi communiter persuasum sit & commentatoribus juris Justinianei & Pragmaticis, actionem nostram esse actionem legis Aquiliæ. Non vero videtur commodius tra-
ctari & ostendi posse assertio nostra, quam si ostendamus:
quid jus Gentium requirat in restitutione damni dati? quid
addiderit aut detraxerit juri Gentium lex Aquilia? quid
rursus immutaverit jus canonicum? quid mores prisci Germanorum hac parte observaverint? quid hodierni? an no-
vi quid introduxerint? Unde orti? quomodo quæstiones
inde dependentes sint definiendæ?

§. II.

Damnum alteri a nobis datum, esse resarciendum, ita
cordibus hominum inscriptum est, ut nemo unquam, quod-
cunque etiam primum Juris Naturæ vel Gentium principi-
um supposuerit, ea de re dubitaverit. Postulat id communis tranquillitas, postulat æqualitas humani generis. Nemo sibi vult damnum dari, non itaque det aliis. Quilibet
vult sibi damnum ab aliis datum resarciri; resarciat aliis.
Suum cuique tribuendum est: tribuatur & damni restitu-
tio. Nemo lædendus. Frustraneum hoc esset præceptum,
si post læsionem non tenerer læso ad satisfactionem.

§. III.

Neque interest, sive deliberato animo alteri damnum
dem, sive non data opera. Uti enim recta ratio dictitat,
dolum meum non debere mihi prodesse nec alteri nocere:
ita eadem est ratio meæ negligentiæ. Nullum est fundamentum, per quod alteri imputare possim negligentiam meam. Ergo si alterutri debet negligentia nocere, æquius
est, ut mihi quam ut alteri. Multæ felicitates mihi accidunt, quas non sum meritus, aut ad quarum acquisitionem
nihil

although it is generally considered both by the commentators on Justinian's Law and by Practitioners that our action is the action of the *lex Aquilia*. Now, it does not seem that my statement can be more conveniently treated and proved than by my showing what[1] the *Ius Gentium* requires for the restitution of damage done, what the *lex Aquilia* had added or subtracted from the *Ius Gentium*, further what changes the Canon Law has brought about, what the ancient customs of the Germans observed in this regard, what is done today, whether anything new has been introduced, whence it has arisen, and how questions depending thereon are to be solved.

§ II

That damage done by us to another is to be made good has been so engraved on the hearts of men that no-one has ever had doubts about it, irrespective of what the first principles of the *Ius Naturale* or the *Ius Gentium* laid down. Common tranquillity demands this as does the equity of the human race. No-one wishes damage to be done him, let him not therefore do damage to others. Whosoever wishes damage done him by others to be made good, let him make good damage done by him to others. "Each man is to be given his due." Let restitution of damage also be given. "No-one is to be injured." This precept would be meaningless if, after committing an injury, I were not liable[2] for compensation to the injured party.

§ III

It is of no importance whether I do damage to another with deliberate intent or unintentionally. For in as much as right reason dictates that my malicious intention ought not to benefit me nor to injure another, so the reason is the same regarding my negligence. There is no basis on which I can impute my own negligence to another. Therefore if my negligence has to injure one of the two of us, it is more equitable that it injures me rather than another. Many blessings befall me, which I have not deserved, or to the acquiring of which

---

[1] In the 1703 edition *quod*
[2] In the 1703 edition *teneret*

nihil contulit induſtria mea. Ergo æquum eſt, ut etiam feram illa, quæ accidunt absque induſtria mea, & propo-ſito.

§. IV.

Quare non ſolum recta ratio ſuadet, ut damnum culpa quacunque datum æque reſarciam, ac ſi dolo idem dederim, ſed & ſi plane nulla mea culpa, verum mero caſu alteri damnum datum ſit, modo a me id fuerit datum. Æquum nonſolum, ſed & juſtum eſt, ut damnum caſu datum reſarciam. Æquum eſt, quia pium & humanum eſt, aliis, quibus etiam non a nobis damnum datum eſt, ex abundantia noſtra ſuccurrere & in ſolatium rerum amiſſarum quædam donare; quanto magis iis, qui facto noſtro damnum paſſi ſunt: Juſtum eſt, quia tranquillitas humani generis id poſtulat. Finge: ſum apud amicum: vitrum aliquod pretioſum adſpicio, manibus id meis circumvolvens: ex improviſo aliquid accidit, quod maximum terrorem non mihi ſaltem, ſed & domino vitri incutit; Terror hic ita me occupat, ut vitrum ex manibus cadat. Quis jam damnum hoc ferre debet? Eſto: non habui intentionem vitrum frangendi, non fui negligens in ejus conſideratione: nihil mihi imputari poteſt, merus caſus eſt. Sed idem adverſus me allegabit Dominus vitri. Neque ego, inquiet, habui intentionem vitrum frangendi; nec ulla negligentia mihi imputari poteſt. Et intuitu mei merus caſus eſt. Quid ergo faciendum? an partienda ſatisfactio inter dominum rei & eum qui cauſa phyſica damni fuit? Non arbitror. Nam quicquid ſit de imputatione ex dolo & negligentia, ſufficit, quod ego damnum dederim, dominus vero ad illud nec phyſice nec moraliter concurrerit. Sufficit, quod factum meum

my diligence has contributed nothing. Therefore it is equitable that I should also bear those mishaps which befall me without my intention or purpose.

§ IV

Therefore right reason argues that I should not only make good damage done because of some negligence on my part just as if I had done the same by deliberate intent, but I should also make it good if damage has been done to another clearly through no fault of mine but by pure accident provided the damage has been done by me. It is not only equitable but even just that I should make good damage done by accident. It is equitable because it is a moral and human obligation to succour others from our abundance, even those to whom damage has not been done by us, and to give something[3] as a *solatium* (consolation) for their loss of property. How much[4] more should we give to those who have suffered loss because of our act. It is just, because the well-being of the human race demands it. Consider, I am at a friend's house. I am looking at some valuable glass, turning it in my hands. Suddenly something happens which greatly startles not only me but also the owner of the glass. I am so startled that the glass falls from my hands. Now who ought to bear this loss? This is the position. I did not have the intention of breaking the glass. I was not negligent in looking at it. Nothing can be laid at my door; it is a pure accident. However, the owner of the glass will allege the same against me. He will say, "I did not have the intention of breaking the glass. No negligence can be laid at my door and, as far as I can judge, it is a pure accident." What then must be done? Must the *satisfactio* (reparation) be divided between the owner of the article and him who was the physical cause of the damage? I do not think so. For whatever is implied about intent or negligence, it suffices that I did the damage, while the owner contributed neither physically nor morally to it. It suffices that the owner can hold my act

---

[3] In 1703 edition *quodam*
[4] In 1703 and 1774 editions *quando*

meum dominus adversus me allegare possit. Nam si vitrum non sumsissem in manus, non etiam id fuisset fractum. Quam innocens igitur sit curiositas mea, mea tamen est, non domini vitri. Ergo justum est, ut qui ex hac innocente curiositate delectationem capio, etiam damnum sentiam, etsi innocenter secutum.

§. V.

Cum tamen in his & similibus casibus, ubi nec ex proposito, nec ex culpa aut negligentia damnum dedi, multæ æque infinitæ possint intervenire circumstantiæ, ut difficile sit definire, quis damnum resarcire debeat; hinc communiter dici solet, quod casum sentiat dominus. Finge: terrorem istum fuisse mihi & reliquis incussum per explosionem sclopeti; dubium esse: utrum alter jus explodendi habuerit: an ex petulantia id fecerit &c. Finge concussione illa aëris, quasdam res, quæ ibi collocatæ erant, unde vitrum sumseram, sua sponte in terram cecidisse, non tamen omnes. Finge: me motu valde præcipitato januam claudere vel aperire; eo motu simul per aëris contactum fenestram non bene clausam & obseratam aperiri; simul vero hoc motu fenestræ quædam perdi vel frangi &c. A quo hic Dominus petet damni dati resarcitionem: quem convincet esse veram causam (saltem physicam) damni dati? Igitur quia omnis actor jure Gentium debet id agere, ut cuilibet tertio appareat fundamentum actionis, & in moralibus idem valet, non esse & non apparere; leges etiam de eo fieri debent, quod non semel aut bis, sed frequenter fit; non iniquum etiam est censendum, quodsi legibus plerarumque Gentium concedatur actio de damno dato resarciendo, adversus eum saltem, qui dolo vel culpa quacunque damnum dederit, non qui casu.

§. VI.

against me. For if I had not taken the glass into my hands, it would not have been broken. Therefore, however innocent my curiosity, it is nevertheless my curiosity, not the curiosity of the owner of the glass. Therefore it is just that I who derived pleasure because of this innocent curiosity should also suffer the loss although it followed without any intent to do harm.

§ V

Since, however, in these and similar cases, where I did damage neither intentionally nor by fault or negligence, many and indeed infinite circumstances can feature so that it is difficult to decide who ought to make good the damage, hence it is customarily said by the world at large that the owner bears the loss for accident. Imagine for instance: that fear which filled me and the others was caused by the firing of a musket. There is doubt whether the party responsible had the right to fire or whether he did it from wantonness, etc. Imagine that because of that agitation of the air, certain articles which had been standing in the place from where I took the glass fell to the ground of their own accord, not however all of them. Imagine that with a sudden and violent movement, I either shut or opened the door; at the same time by that movement because of the rush of air, a window which was not properly shut and fastened opened, and at the same time because of this movement certain panes were smashed or broken, etc. From whom will this owner claim the restitution of the damage done? Whom will he prove to be the true cause (at least the physical cause) of the damage done? And so because every plaintiff, in terms of the *Ius Gentium*, has to claim something in such a way that the basis of the action appears clear to any third party, and in moral matters "not being" and "not appearing to be" have the same effect. For laws ought to be made about a situation which occurs not once or twice but frequently. It is not to be considered unfair if an action for the making good of damage done is granted by the laws of most countries only against him who did damage because of some malicious intent or negligence, not against him who did it by accident.

§. VI.

Porro uti regulae aequitatis & humanitatis volunt, ut, ubi apertum est, duos dolose invicem insidiis, aut sibi damnum dedisse, ut dolus cum dolo compensetur, & sic uterque damnum, quod plusquam sua culpa fuerit, ferat; ita non multum absimilis ratio est, si concurrat culpa Domini cum culpa damnum dantis. In quo enim defectu humanae naturae quisque cum altero concurrit, ibi non aequum est, ut propter illum defectum ab altero aliquid acquirere velit. Ex hac regula aequitatis sua sponte fluit, quod, si apud negligentem in suis rebus amicum res meas deposuerim, aut ei custodiendas tradiderim, qui in propriis rebus custodiendis non multum diligens est; aut quod si cum tali homine negligente societatem iniverim; mihi imputare debeam, si damnum in re deposita, vel ad societatem pertinente datum fuerit, modo is tum res suas non melius observaverit, aut custodierit, ubi dolus apertus vel certe ab omnibus praesumtus adest.

§. VII.

Itaque facile exinde cognoscitur, quod jure Gentium, etiamsi dixerimus, eum qui casu damnum physice dedit ad reparationem teneri, tamen illa assertio inde quoque limitationem accipiat, si Dominus ipse rei simul causa vel saltem occasio damni dati fuerit: v. gr. si amico vitrum illud pretiosum considerandum ipse in manus dederit; si petat ab amico, ut vitrum istud in alto loco collocatum inde auferat, & amicus casu de scammo cadat &c.

§. VIII.

Porro Jure Gentium in actione de damno dato nihil probandum est ulterius, quam quod reus damnum dederit,

B   utrum

§ VI

Furthermore as the rules of human equity require that, in as much as when it is clear that when two men intentionally injured each other or did damage to each other's property so that intent may be offset by intent and thus each may bear the loss which he suffered from in excess of his own fault, so the reasoning is not very different if the negligence of the owner runs concurrently with the negligence of the one doing the damage. For there is nothing to choose between them as far as this human failing is concerned and in this case it is not fair that because of that failing one should wish to acquire something from the other. And from this rule of equity it automatically follows that if I deposit my property with a friend who is negligent with regard to his own property or give it into the care of one who is not very careful in looking after his own property, or if I have joined in partnership with such a negligent man, I ought to blame myself if damage is done to the article deposited or to the property belonging to the partnership, provided that my friend or partner did not look after or care for his own property better than mine. If such is the case it is clear, or at least assumed by everyone, that intent is present.

§ VII

And so it is easily learned from this that even if, in terms of the *Ius Gentium*, we say that he who physically did the damage by accident is liable for reparation, nevertheless that statement may require certain qualifications if the owner himself was at the same time the cause of the act or at least provided the occasion for the damage done; for example, if he himself had put the valuable glass into his friend's hands so that he could look at it, or if he asked his friend to take the glass from the high place where it was standing and his friend by chance fell from the stool[5], etc.

§ VIII

Further by the *Ius Gentium* in the action for damage done nothing more must be proved than that the accused did the damage,

---

[5] In the 1703 edition *scamno*

utrum dolo vel negligentia id factum fuerit, non probandum est, quia quoad restitutionem damni dati hic nihil interest, quod vero in quæstionem non venit, ejus probatione actor non est onerandus. Nec obest, quod reus excipere possit, se nec dolo nec culpa dedisse damnum, sed mero casu, adeoque hoc intuitu omnino dolus aut culpa dantis damnum veniet in quæstionem. Præterquam enim, quod jam docuerimus, Jure Gentium regulariter obligari damnum dantem etiam in infortunio vel casu; posito etiam, quod tales concurrant circumstantiæ, quæ reum a restitutione damni liberent, aut quod lege civili id cautum sit, ut casu dans damnum non conveniri efficaciter possit, sufficit, quod hic præsumtionem pro se habeat actor, cum plerumque, & ita regulariter, damna fiant culpa dantium. Actor vero, qui præsumtionem pro se habet, a probatione liberatur, & quoties porro Actor se in regula fundat, reus in exceptione, probatio tum non actori, sed reo ex natura rei & sic ex Jure Gentium incumbit.

§. IX.

Jam vero evidens est, quid Jure Gentium sentiendum sit de eo casu, si furiosus aut infans damnum dederit. Quilibet homo alteri resarcire debet damnum, quod dedit. Excipit furiosus vel infans: ego non restituo, quia furiosus vel infans sum. Quæ ratio connexionis? Atqui nec doli nec culpæ sum capax. Capax tamen es, ut damnum dare possis. Furor tuus est: Infantia tua est, ergo ad te etiam pertinent omnia, quæ ex furore & infantia sequuntur. Quæ enim ulla ratio suadere potest, ut furor & infantia tua non tibi, sed mihi noceat. Quoties obligatio ex re venit, i. e. ex æquitate naturali, non ex contractu, neque ex delicto, toties
etiam

not whether it was done with intent or negligence, because, with regard to the restitution of damage done, nothing is here of importance which does not in truth come into that question and the plaintiff is not to be burdened with proof thereof. Nor is there an obstacle in the fact that the accused can offer the *exceptio* that he did not cause the damage by intent or negligence but by pure accident and therefore that, on this basis certainly, the intent or negligence of the one doing the damage does come into question. For in addition to what we have already stated, namely that by the *Ius Gentium* the one doing damage even by ill fortune or accident is regularly liable, assuming also that such circumstances may occur as to free the accused from restitution of the damage done or that in the Civil Law it is provided that one doing damage by chance cannot be successfully sued, it suffices that here the plaintiff has the presumption in his favour, since generally, and thus regularly, damage is done because of the negligence of the doer. Moreover the plaintiff who has this presumption in his favour is freed from proof and indeed whenever the plaintiff takes his stand on a rule, and the accused on an *exceptio*, then the burden of proof lies not on the plaintiff but on the accused because of the nature of the situation and it is so in terms of the *Ius Gentium*.

§ IX

But now it is clear as to what must be decided in terms of the *Ius Gentium* about the case where a madman or an infant has done damage. Everyone ought to make good to another the damage which he did. However the madman or an infant says by way of defence "I do not make restitution because I am mad or because I am an infant." "What is the logical connection?" "Because I am capable neither of intent nor negligence." "However you are capable of doing damage. The madness is yours, the infancy is yours. Therefore to you also pertain all those things which follow on madness or infancy. For what reason is there for your madness and your infancy injuring me but not you?" Whenever an obligation arises from a thing, i.e. from natural equity, not from contract or from delict, then

etiam obligantur furiosi & infantes. Jure Gentium actio
datur ob damnum injuria datum. Injuria vero in materia
damni dati omne denotat, quod non fit jure. Sufficit ergo,
quod furiosus infans nullum jus habeat damni mihi dandi,
& ideo, quia nullum jus habet, obligatus etiam est ad damni
a se dati restitutionem. Quid putas? furiosus & infans
vult mihi damnum dare, nondum dedit: sum ne obligatus,
ut patiar, damnum mihi dari? An impedire id possum?
Possum utique. Sed urget furiosus. Possum resistere,
possum repellere, etiam verberibus, si opus sit, & adhibita
vi majore. Quia videlicet furiosus nullum jus habet dandi damnum, ego vero jus habeo defendendi rem meam.
Ego, qui jure meo utor, furioso non facio injuriam. Furiosus etsi furiosus, cum nullum jus habeat, injuriam mihi
facit. Igitur cum possim furiosum, etiam cum gravi damno
corpori ejus illato, repellere, cur non possim petere restitutionem damni dati ex bonis ejus?

§. X.

Sequitur porro ex dictis, fontem actionis de reparatione damni Jure Gentium non magis esse delictum alterius,
quam contractum, quia hic non consideratur, an alter intentionem habuerit damni dandi nec ne. Delicta vero ex intentione judicantur. Unde saepius diximus, actionem hanc
ex aequitate oriri. Ne tamen urgeas; aequitatem hanc vi-
deri cerebrinam, nisi fons specialior ostendatur, dicam, quod
sentio. Damni in re sua dati reparationem petere ex Dominio fluit. Dum enim res jure Dominii fit propria, non
solum Dominus de ejus rei usu regulariter disponere, alios
pro lubitu ab eo excludere, vel ad illum admittere potest,
sed & rem vindicare, alienare, conservare, defendere, & igitur de damno etiam in ea dato satisfactionem petere.

B 2 §. XI.

also madmen and infants are liable. The action from the *Ius Gentium* is given for damage done unlawfully. Unlawfully in the context of damage done denotes everything which is not done lawfully. It suffices, therefore, that a madman or[6] an infant has no right to do damage to me and therefore, because he has no right, he is also liable for restitution of the damage done by him. What do you think? A madman or an infant wishes to do damage to me, he has not yet done it. Am I obliged to suffer that damage be done me? Am I allowed to prevent it? I am indeed. But the madman presses on. I can resist, I can drive him away, even with blows if necessary and by using greater force. For, of course, a madman has no right to do damage, whereas I do have a right to defend my property. I, who am exercising my right, am not doing an injury to the madman; the madman, even if he is mad, is doing me an injury since he has no such right. Therefore since I am able to repel the madman even by inflicting grave physical injury on him, why should I not be able to claim restitution from his property for the damage done me?

§ X

It follows further from what has been said that the basis of the action for reparation of damage in terms of the *Ius Gentium* is no more the other party's delict than it is his contract, because here there is no question of whether the other had the intention of doing damage or not, for delicts are judged from intent. Hence we have more than once said that this action is based on equity. Lest however you press on saying, "This equity of yours seems but a figment of the imagination, unless a more specific source is indicated." let me say what I think. To seek reparation for damage done to one's own property flows from ownership. For while a thing belongs to the owner by right of ownership, he is not only normally able to make arrangements for the using of it, to exclude others from it or to admit them to it at his pleasure but he can also vindicate, alienate, preserve or defend it and therefore he can also seek satisfaction for damage done with regard to it.

---

[6] In the 1703 edition *et*

§. IX.

Hinc & regulariter actio de damno reparando non alii danda est quam Domino rei, quia tamen factum alterius semper præsupponit, etiam Jure Gentium non ad actiones reales, sed personales est referenda; neque etiam actor hic de probando Dominio tantopere debet esse sollicitus, quia a reo ipsi de Dominio non movetur controversia, & quando dictum fuit, Domino dari hanc actionem, id non tam intuitu rei, quam tertii concurrentis intelligendum est, ut huic præferatur Dominus rei.

§. XII.

Dum vero reparationem damni dati hic petimus, res ipsa ostendit, nos petere id, quod nobis abest, i. e. æstimationem damni dati. Unde hæc actio Jure Gentium non nisi rei persecutoria est. Dum enim, ut ostensum, a dolo vel culpa damnum dantis abstrahitur, pœnam vero sola delicta dolo data requirunt, certe negligentia minimi gradus, qualis tamen ab hac actione non excusat, omnem pœnam respuit: qua ex ratione Dominus damnum patiens posset pœnam ab altero exigere? Porro dum ex Dominio fluit eadem actio, nulla ratio subest pœnam exigens. Uti enim, dum alter rem meam detinet, nihil aliud quam substantiam rei ejusque fructus vindico; ita si substantia rei læsa est, aut lucrum certum rei interceptum, nil nisi valorem rei & æstimationem, postulo, & quidem, cum pretia rei varient, valorem qui fuit tempore dati, hactenus enim saltem mihi damnum datum fuit.

§. XIII.

Cum vero heres secundum mores Gentium succedat in omnia debita defuncti, minimum eo usque quatenus ad

eorum

§ XI [7]

Hence also normally the action for making good damage is not granted to anyone other than to the owner of the article, however, because it always presupposes an act on the part of another and, even in terms of the *Ius Gentium*, it must be classified not with real actions, but with personal actions. Now even here the plaintiff here must not be greatly concerned about proving ownership because this is not a dispute about ownership brought by the accused against him, and whenever it is said "this action is granted to the owner", this must be understood not so much with regard to the accused but with regard to a third party also claiming, so that the owner of the article is given preference.

§ XII

But when we here claim reparation for damage done, it is self-evident that we claim what we have lost, that is the value of the damage done. Hence this action in terms of the *Ius Gentium* is only reipersecutory. For while, as shown, the action is divorced from the intent or negligence of the person who has done the damage, and since only delicts committed with intent require punishment, and certainly negligence in a minor degree, although such as does not exonerate from this action, rejects all punishment, on what grounds can an owner suffering loss demand a penalty from the other party? Further, while this same action stems from ownership, no rationale for demanding punishment exists. For when another retains my property, I claim nothing other than the substance of the article and its fruits, thus if the substance of the article has been damaged, or the definite gain of the article has been intercepted, I claim nothing except the value of the article and an evaluation of the definite gain and indeed since the value of articles may vary, I claim the value which it had at the time of the damage done, for thus far only was damage done to me.

§ XIII

But since an heir, according to the customs of the nations, succeeds to all the debts of the deceased, at least in as far as the estate of the deceased suffices for

---

[7] Reading *XI* for *IX* as in the 1703 edition

eorum folutionem-fufficiant bona defuncti; hinc Jure Gentium nullum est dubium, quod heredes damnum dantis teneantur etiam ad ejus reparationem. Nulla enim ratio exceptionis hic adest, cur non debeant obligati esse.

§. XIV.

Quodsi etiam plures damnum dederint, id certum est, si constet, ad quam partem damni quis concurrerit, singulos non de toto damno, sed quemque de sua parte teneri. Quodsi non constet, etsi varii casus possint oriri, ut singuli teneantur in solidum, quos hic discutere non est hujus loci, nullum tamen est dubium, quin Jure Gentium unius præstatione reliqui liberentur, quia tum videlicet dominus rei æstimationem quæ ipsi aberat jam habet.

§. XV.

Habes ita naturam actionis de reparatione damnorum ex Jure Gentium. Quod nullos autores hic citaverim, ægre non feres. Cum enim Jus Gentium naturalis ratio dictitet omnibus hominibus, & speremus etiam, lectores sua ratione, non commodata aut precario rogata præditos fore, noluimus illis tanquam in re plana, tædium creare, allegatione magnorum virorum, quos alias veneramur, aut etiam nominum barbarorum, Moralistarum videlicet vel Italorum vel Hispanorum, quibus mulieres in Indiis infantes terrere solent.

§. XVI.

Jam videndum, quid lex Aquilia Juris Gentium dispositioni addiderit, vel detraxerit. Ubi præstabit rem ex fontibus ostendere magis quam ex rivis Systematum, aut cloacis Glossatorum. *Lex Aquilia*, ait ULPIANUS, *l. 1. ff. h. t. omnibus legibus, quæ ante se de damno injuria locuta sunt, de-*

roga-

the payment thereof, consequently in terms of the *Ius Gentium,* there is no doubt that the heirs of one who has done damage are also liable for its reparation. For no grounds for an exception as to why they ought not to be liable are here present.

§ XIV

But if several people did damage, it is certain that, if it is established what amount of the damage each contributed, individually they are not liable for the whole damage but each is liable for his part. But, if it is not established, even if various situations can arise such that several individuals may be liable for the whole (it is not the place to discuss these here), nevertheless there is no doubt that by the *Ius Gentium* when one man pays the rest are absolved from payment, because then indeed the owner of the article already has the value which was lost to him.

§ XV

Thus you have the nature of the action for the reparation of damage in terms of the *Ius Gentium.* You will not take it amiss that here I have cited no authorities. For since natural reason dictates the *Ius Gentium* to all men and since we would also hope that our readers will be blessed with reason, their own, not borrowed or requested as a *precarium* (loan on request), we were unwilling to bore them in so easy a matter by the naming of great men whom we otherwise deeply respect or even by the citing of foreign-sounding names, namely, the names of the Moral Philosophers, be they Italian or Spanish, bogeymen with whom women in the Indies are wont to frighten their infants.

§ XVI

Now we must see what the *lex Aquilia* adds or subtracts from the disposition of the *Ius Gentium.* Here it will be best to present the material from the source rather than from the runnels of the Systematists[8] or the sewers of the Glossators. Ulpian says (D. 9, 2, 1, pr.):

The *lex Aquilia*[9] derogated all laws which previously dealt[10] with unlawful damage

---

[8] *Systematum* is a genitive plural of συστημα - ατος. It could also be a typesetting error for *systematicorum.* Probably the writers of the Natural Law Systems are mere meant, e.g. Pufendorf. Alternatively he means Academics generally.

[9] For *Les* reading *lex* as in the 1703 edition

[10] For *locuta sunt* reading *locutae sunt* as in the 1703 edition

rogavit, five duodecim tabulis, five alia qua fuit. Quas leges nunc referre non est necesse. Quænam fuerint illæ priscæ leges, quibus derogaverit lex Aquilia, nec ad scopum nostrum pertinet, nec poterimus etiam distinctius multo indagare, cum ea ignorare nos voluerit diligentia Justiniani. Interim, uti illud certum, quod Romani semper, & adeo diu ante legem Aquiliam habuerint actiones de damno dato, ita verosimile est, eas magis convenisse cum Jure Gentium hactenus exposito, cum lex Aquilia iis omnibus derogaverit, uti derogavit fere omnibus hactenus recensitis Juris Gentium capitibus. Quemadmodum vero plane impertinens foret, si actiones illas antiquas Juris Romani de damno dato vellemus appellare actiones legis Aquiliæ antiquas, cum lex Aquilia iis derogaverit; ita æque impertinens erit, si quis actiones alterius Gentis ab actione legis Aquiliæ essentialiter discrepantes, velit actionem legis Aquiliæ essentialiter discrepantes, velit actionem legis Aquiliæ ex eo solum dicere, quod in iis agatur de damno dato.

§. XVII.

Lege Aquilia primo capite cavetur, ut qui servum, servamve, alienum, alienamve, quadrupedem, vel pecudem, injuria occiderit: quanti id in eo anno plurimi fuit, tantum æs dare Domino damnas esto. (GAJUS *l. 2. pr. ad L. Aquil.*) *Hujus legis secundum quidem capitulum in desuetudinem abiit. Tertio autem capite ait eadem lex Aquilia: Cæterarum rerum, præter hominem & pecudem occisos, si quis alteri damnum faxit, quod usserit, fregerit, ruperit injuria: quanti ea res erit in diebus triginta proximis, tantum æs domino dare damnas esto.* (ULPIANUS *l. 27. §. 4. & 5. ff. eod.*) *Hæc verba: quanti in triginta diebus proximis fuit, etsi non ha-*
bent

be it the law of the XII Tables or any other which existed. It is now not necessary to refer to these laws.

What these old laws were which the *lex Aquilia* derogated does not pertain to the scope of our work nor would we be able to investigate them with any degree of clarity since the diligence of Justinian insured we should be ignorant of them. Meanwhile in as much as it is certain that the Romans always, and so for a long time before the *lex Aquilia,* had actions for damage done, consequently it is very likely that these accorded quite closely with the *Ius Gentium,* as explained above, since the *lex Aquilia* derogated all those laws, as it derogated almost all the basic principles of the *Ius Gentium,* as hitherto reviewed. Thus it would clearly be inappropriate if we were to call those ancient Roman Law actions for damage done "the ancient actions of the *lex Aquilia*", because the *lex Aquilia* derogated them. Thus it would be equally inapposite if anyone were to say that the actions of some other nation, differing in essence from the *lex Aquilia*[11], were the action of the *lex Aquilia* solely because damage done is treated therein.

§ XVII

In the first chapter of the *lex Aquilia* it is provided that he who has unlawfully killed another's male or female slave, or his quadruped, that is a head of cattle, shall be liable to pay to the owner as much as it was worth at most in that year (Gaius D. 9, 2, 2, pr.). Indeed the second chapter of this law has fallen into desuetude. Further in the third chapter the same *lex Aquilia* says: if anyone has done damage to another with regard to any other property, with the exception of killing a man or beast, by unlawfully burning, breaking or spoiling it, he shall be liable to pay to the owner as much money as that thing will be worth in the next 30 days (Ulpian D. 9, 2, 27, 4; D. 9, 2, 27, 5). Although these words "how much it will be worth in the next 30 days" do not include the word

---

[11] The repetition of the words *velit...discrepantes* is a typesetting error. This does not occur in the 1703 edition.

bent plurimi, sic tamen esse accipienda constat, (ULPIANUS
l. 29. §. sin. ff. eod.)

§. XVIII.

Jam in confesso apud omnes est, quod lex Aquilia in
eo a Jure Gentium recesserit, quod non voluerit simplicem
damni dati aestimationem domino restitui, quanti videlicet
res fuerit tempore damni dati, sed quanti plurimi retro fuerit vel in anno, quando mancipium aut quadrupes fuerint
occisae, vel in mense seu proximis triginta diebus, in reliquis
damnorum speciebus. Et in hoc consistit formalis & es-
sentialis ratio legis Aquiliae. Quemadmodum vero ratio
differentiae inter primum & tertium caput; & cur diversae
praestationes ibi fuerint injunctae, forte non difficulter dari
posset; Ita non diffitendum est, longe difficilius esse, genui-
nam rationem invenire, quae moverit Aquillium, ut plus
quam damni revera dati reparationem, injunxerit damnum
dantibus. Divinatoribus hic nobis esse non licet, nec ad
scopum nostrum pertinet. Circumstantiis tamen omnibus
probe expensis nil convenientius dici poterit, quam duram
quidem esse legem, ita tamen scriptam.

§. XIX.

Quodsi Aquilius dolum eorum, qui damna dederunt,
coërcere voluisset, res nullum haberet dubium; At cum
hic a dolo abstrahatur, & aeque actio legis Aquiliae detur, si
vel minima negligentia damnum fuerit datum, & quoad
hanc circumstantiam requisita juris Gentium *supra §. 2. & 3.*
annotata, intempestive fuerint retenta, in occulto adhuc
manet aequitas legis Aquiliae. *Injuriam* (inquit ULPIANUS
l. 5. §. 1. h. t.) *hic accipere nos oportet: non quemadmodum
circa injuriarum actionem, contumeliam quandam: sed quod
non*

'plurimi' (at most) nevertheless it is agreed that it must be understood (Ulpian D. 9, 2, 29, 8).

§ XVIII

Now it is agreed among all that the *lex Aquilia* departed from the *Ius Gentium* in that it did not wish the simple estimation of the damage done to be restored to the owner, namely as much as the property was worth at the time of the damage done but, when a slave or four-footed beast had been killed, it wished the owner to be paid the highest value that the property had attained during the preceding year, and in the case of all other forms of damage, the highest value during the past month or thirty days. In this consists the formal and essential rationale of the *lex Aquilia*. But although the reason for the difference between the first and third chapters and why different provisions were there laid down could perhaps be given without difficulty, it cannot be denied that it is much more difficult to find the true reason which prompted Aquilius to lay on those doing damage reparation of more than the damage actually done. We may not here indulge in guesswork, nor does it pertain to our purpose. And so when all factors have been duly assessed, nothing can more aptly be said than "indeed the law is harsh but thus it is written."

§ XIX

But if Aquilius had wished to punish the intent of those who did damage, then there would be no doubt. But since here he does not stay with intent and the action under the *lex Aquilia* is given equally if the damage was done because of very slight negligence and thus with regard to this aspect, the requirements of the *Ius Gentium* mentioned above in §§ 2 and 3 were unreasonably restricted, the equity of the *lex Aquilia* still remains unclear. Ulpian says (D. 9, 2, 5, 1):

Of course, we must not here take *'iniuria'* to mean some sort of insult as in the *actio iniuriarum*, but as meaning that which

non jure factum est, hoc est, contra jus, id est, sir culpa quis occiderit, & ideo interdum utraque actio concurrit, & legis Aquiliæ & injuriarum. Sed duæ erunt æstimationes, alia damni, alia contumeliæ. Igitur injuriam hic damnum accipiemus culpa datum, etiam ab eo, qui nocere noluit. PAULUS *(l. 30. f. 3. eod.) In hac quoque actione, quæ ex hoc capitulo (tertio) oritur, dolus & culpa punitur.* Rursus ULPIANUS *(l. 44. pr. eod.) In lege Aquilia & levissima culpa venit.*

§. XX.

Porro, uti & in eo Lex Aquilia non recessit a Jure Gentium, quod soli Domino voluerit actionem dari, *l. 11. f. 6. eodem (conf. supra f. 11.)* ita & similiter verius est, si quis in re, quam ex contractu penes se habet, damnum non ea culpa dederit, quam ex natura contractus præstare tenetur, non solum cessare actionem ex contractu, sed etiam actionem Legis Aquiliæ, quia videlicet hic culpa Domini concurrit per dicta superius *f. 6.* & quia contradictionem involveret, ad diligentiam aliquem ex contractu non teneri, ne quidem ad simplicem rei æstimationem præstandam, & tamen ex lege Aquilia teneri ad duriorem æstimationem. *Illustris* DN. STRYKE *in Usu Moderno ad tit. de L. Aquil. f. 14. & in tractatu de action. investig. Sect. I. membr. 10. f. 28.* Unde facile satisfieri poterit rationibus dissentientium; quod lex Aquilia non sit subsidiarium remedium uti actio doli, sed ordinarium, & contractus interveniens non possit majorem delinquendi licentiam tribuere contrahentibus, quam aliis. Neque enim sequitur: actio legis Aquiliæ est remedium ordinarium, ergo contrahentes ea possunt conveniri. Et quia in Lege Aquilia non opus est ulla probatione doli vel culpæ ab altero commissæ, ac culpa etiam delictum non

consti-

is done unlawfully, that is contrary to law, e.g. if someone has killed negligently. Thus although from time to time the action of the *lex Aquilia* and the *actio iniuriarum* concur, there will in such a case be two evaluations, one for the wrongful damage, the other for the insult. Therefore we shall here understand '*iniuria*' as damage done in a blameworthy fashion, even by one who did not wish to do harm.

Paul says (D. 9, 2, 30, 3) "also in the action with arises from this (third) chapter both intent and negligence are punished." Further Ulpian says (D. 9, 2, 44, pr.) "even very trifling negligence falls under the *lex Aquilia*."

§ XX

Further as the *lex Aquilia* does not deviate from the *Ius Gentium* in that it wishes the action to be granted to the owner alone (D. 9, 2, 11, 6; compare § 11 above) so too it is similarly sound law that if someone does damage to an article which he has in his possession as a result of a contract, but not with the degree of negligence for which he is liable in terms of the contract, not only is the action *ex contractu* void but also the action under the *lex Aquilia* because, of course, there is concurrent fault on the part of the owner, according to what was said above in § 6, and because it would involve a contradiction to hold someone not liable for *diligentia* in terms of a contract - not even to make good the simple value of the article - and then to hold him liable for the harsher evaluation in terms of the *lex Aquilia* (Stryk, *Usus Modernus Pandectarum, ad* D. 9, 2, 14; *De Actione Investigatione*, 1. 10. 28). Hence the arguments of those who disagree can easily be met, namely that the *lex Aquilia* is not a subsidiary remedy like the *actio doli*, but a regular remedy and the existence of a contract cannot attribute more freedom to commit an offence to the contracting parties than to other people. For this does not follow: the *actio Legis Aquiliae* is a regular remedy and therefore contracting parties make agreements concerning it. And because in the *lex Aquilia* there is no need for any proof of intent or negligence committed by the other party and even negligence does not

conftituit, hinc etiam non poteft inferri ex fententia noftra, quod hoc pacto contrahentibus major delinquendi licentia fuppeditetur.

§. XXI.

Jam cum Lex Aquilia reum condemnaverit quidem in rei æftimationem, fed *quanti retro plurimi fuerit*, quod fatis irregulare & durum fuiffe oftendimus; peperit hæc capitalis irregularitas alias plures. Incertum enim erat & valde dubium, an hæc actio debeat annumerari actionibus rei perfecutoriis? quia fimplex rei æftimatio petitur; an pœnalibus? quia petitur non veri damni reftitutio, fed reus condemnatur in majus, quanti fcilicet res retro fuerit; an mixtis? quia tamen hæc condemnatio continebat in fe reftitutionem veri pretii. Quemadmodum ergo JCti veteres facile inter fe diffentiebant, utpote variis fectis dediti; ita nullum eft dubium, diffenfiffe & in hac quæftione. ULPIANUS eam pro pœnali habet *l. 11. §. 2. l. 23. §. §. h. t.* Et hujus fententiam JUSTINIANUS recepit in Pandectis an recte, jam non difputo. Nec difputo an eum intellexerit? Ulpianum enim habuiffe actionem L. Aquiliæ pro mere pœnali docebunt fequentia. Contra Juftinianus habuit pro actione mixta *in Inftit. §. 19. de actionibus.*

§. XXII.

Referamus faltem rationes, quæ pro fententia ULPIANI afferri poffunt. Eas fuppeditat DN. SCHILTER *Exerc. ad Pandect. 19. tb. 47. Atque,* inquit, *cum & fimplum pœnam contineat, ideo creditum eft,* ait JUSTIANUS *§. 9. h. t. pœnalem effe bujus legis actionem, quia non folum tanti quisque obligatur, quantum damni dederit, fed aliquando longe pluris. Ideoque conftat, in beredem eam actionem non tranfire, quæ*

C

tranfi-

constitute the delict, hence it cannot be inferred from our view that by virtue of this agreement the contracting parties are provided with greater freedom for committing an offence.

§ XXI

Now, since the *lex Aquilia* condemned the accused for the value of the article and indeed for "the highest value that the property attained retrospectively", and this we have shown was very irregular and harsh, this basic irregularity was father to several others. For it was uncertain and indeed very questionable whether this action ought to be included among reipersecutory actions, because the simple value of the article is claimed or, should it be included among penal actions, because it is not restitution of actual damage that is claimed but the accused is condemned for more, namely for (the highest) value that the property attained retrospectively or, should it be classified with mixed actions, on the grounds that this condemnation nonetheless contains within itself restitution of the true value? Therefore as the ancient Jurists readily disagreed with each other, being members of various schools of thought, so there is no doubt that they disagreed on this question too. Ulpian (D. 9, 2, 11, 2; D. 9, 2, 23, 8) considers the action penal. And Justinian took over his view in the Digest - whether rightly, I am not now discussing. Nor am I discussing whether Justinian understood Ulpian correctly, for the following fragments of the *Digest* will show that Ulpian considered the action of the *lex Aquilia* as purely penal. On the other hand, in the *Institutes* 4, 6, 19 Justinian considers it a mixed action.

§ XXII

Let us at least mention the reasons which can be brought forward in favour of Ulpian's view. Schilter provides these in *Exercitatio ad Pandectas* 19, §.48.[12] He says,

> Since even the simple value includes a penalty it is believed, I quote Justinian[13] (*Inst.* 4 , 3, 9), "that the action of this law is penal because someone is liable not only for as much damage as he did but sometimes for very much more. And therefore it is established that this action does not transfer to the heir. It would have

---

[12] Not 47 but 48
[13] Reading *Justinianus* for *Justianus*

transitura fuisset, si ultra damnum nunquam lis æstimaretur.
Nec errare nos faciet, quod aliquando pluris obligari, quis di-
citur: nam illud non ea intentione dictum accipi debet, quasi
hanc naturalem aptitudinem pluris obligandi non haberet per-
petuam; SCHNEIDEWIN. l. h. t. §. his autem verbis.
TREUTL. I. 18 10. H. PISTOR. l. qu. 27. *sed duntaxat ex-*
ternum illius effectum, atque eventum persecutionis respicit,
non essentiam & naturam obligationis, quam si attendimus,
verum est, regulariter & semper obligari reum in id, quanti
plurimi in eo anno fuerit, non quanti tempore dati damni est:
quod si accidit, ut æstimatio maxima in tempus damni dati
incidat, id accidentale quid est, nec alterat essentiam obligatio-
nis & actionis.   Atque huc facit, quod, ut Hottomannus ar-
bitratur, Tullius appellet hanc plurimi æstimationem MUL-
CTAM L. AQUILIÆ, cum in Bruto ait: atque eodem
tempore accusator de plebe L. Cæsidenus fuit, quem ego audivi
jam senem, cum ab L. Sabelio multam Lege Aquilia de justi-
tia petivisset.   Ubi pro de justitia vult legi damni injuria.
Noluimus autem prolixe examinare has rationes pro sententia Ulpianea allatas.   Nam ut reliqua taceam, quilibet
videt, quod probent saltem, actionem Legis Aquiliæ non
esse unquam mere rei persecutoriam, non vero probant,
quod sit pure pœnalis, ut voluit Ulpianus.

§. XXIII.

Quamvis vero Justinianus sub titulo de Lege Aquilia
saltem Ulpiani sententiam retulerit, actionem hanc pro pœnali habens, reliquorum ex diversis Sectis aliter sentientium
omiserit, alibi tamen incaute retulit etiam sententiam eorum,
qui pro rei persecutoria habuerunt, inter quos fuit eviden-
ter PAULUS, cujus doctrinam excerpsit Tribonianus *in titu-*
lo

transferred if the suit was never valued at more than the amount of the damage." The fact that the defendant is said to be liable for more sometimes will not lead us astray. For that remark ought not to be understood to the effect that it is only sometimes that this action renders the defendant liable for more[14], whereas it always had a natural aptitude for rendering liable for more (see Schneidewinus, *ad Inst.* 4, 3, § *his autem verbis*; Treutler, *Disputationes, lib.* 1, *disp.* 18, § 10 and Pistoris, *Quaestiones, qu.* 27). But that remark refers purely to the external effects thereof and the outcome of the prosecution, not to the essence and nature of the obligation; if we look to that it is true that regularly and always the accused is liable for the highest value the property attained in that year not for as much as it was worth at the time of the damage done. But if it happened that the highest value occurred at the time of the damage done, that is something coincidental, and it does not alter the essence of the obligation and of the action. And hence it comes about that, as Hotman thinks, Cicero calls this assessment of the highest value 'The fine of the *lex Aquilia*' when in the *Brutus* (34. 131) he says "and at the same time there was L. Caesidenus, a man of plebeian rank and a professional accuser whom I heard when he was already an old man. He was trying to get L. Sabelius rendered liable to the fine of the *lex Aquilia* for unlawful damage.[15] There he wanted 'unlawful damage' to be read for 'justice'."

However, we do not want to examine at length these arguments brought forward in favour of Ulpian's view. For to pass over the rest, anyone can see that they prove at least that the action of the *lex Aquilia* was not ever purely reipersecutory, but they do not prove that it was entirely penal, as Ulpian would have it.

§ XXIII

But although under the rubric of the *lex Aquilia* Justinian cited only the opinion of Ulpian who considered this action as penal and omitted the opinion of the others from the opposing schools who thought differently, however here and there he unwittingly also introduced the opinions of those who considered it reipersecutory. Among these was clearly Paul. Tribonian excerpted his theory in the title

---

[14] Schilter has *aliquando...*
[15] Hotman reads *damni iniuria* for the *iustitia* of Cicero's text. See the next sentence.

lo pro focio. *Poftquam enim* ᴜʟᴘɪᴀɴᴜꜱ *l.* *47.* *ſ.1.ff. pro ſo-
cio dixiſſet; *ſocium ſi damnum in re communi dederit, Aqui-*
lia teneri ſecundum opinionem Celſi, Juliani & Pomponii;
additur ſtatim *in l. 48.* ex Paulo, *quod nihilominus & pro ſo-*
cio teneatur, & *in l. 50.* continuatur: *Sed aƈtione pro ſocio*
conſequitur, ut altera aƈtione contentus eſſe debeat, quia utra-
que aƈtio ad rei perſecutionem reſpicit, non, ut furti, ad pænam
duntaxat. Ex eadem hypotheſi ᴘᴀᴜʟɪ eſt *lex 18. ff. h. t.*
etſi hic ſententiæ de natura aƈtionis nulla fiat mentio. *Sed*
etſi is, inquit, *qui pignori ſervum accepit, occidit eum, vel*
vulneravit, lege Aquilia & pignoratitia conveniri poteſt. Sed
alterutra contentus eſſe debebit aƈtor. Habes igitur hic no-
vum exemplum antinomiæ in Jure Juſtinianeo. Scio equidem, quod ᴅɴ. ꜱᴄʜɪʟᴛᴇʀ *d. Exerc. 19. ad Pandeƈt. th. 43.*
conciliare velit Paulum cum Ulpiano, quod videlicet Paulus
non excludat pœnam. Quemadmodum vero ea conciliatio
fundata videtur *in d. l. 50. pro ſocio* verbis: *non, ut furti ad*
pænam duntaxat ; ita rurſus conjeƈtura altera fortior eſt,
quod ᴘᴀᴜʟᴜꜱ *in d. l. 50. & d. l. 18.* aƈtionem legis Aquiliæ præ
mere rei perſecutoria habuerit, quia Paulus ſtatuit, aƈtionem
ex contraƈtu & aƈtionem legis Aquiliæ unam alteram tolle,
re. Si enim legis Aquiliæ aƈtionem habuiſſet pro mixta,
dixiſſet, quod aƈtionem ex Lege Aquilia aƈtio pro ſocio vel
pignoratitia tollat, niſi quatenus illa pinguior eſt, & pœnam
quoque continet. Sed etiamſi demus, Paulum habuiſſe
aƈtionem legis Aquiliæ pro mixta, (quod tamen per diƈta
non videtur) maneret tamen contradiƈtio, quia Ulpianus
eam habuit pro mere pœnali, quemadmodum præter haƈte-
nus diƈta, id latius patebit ex ſequentibus.

C 2   §. XXIV.

Pro Socio (D. 17, 2, 48). For after Ulpian, in D. 17, 2, 47,.1, had said that if a partner had done damage to joint property, he was liable under the *lex Aquilia* according to the opinion of Celsus, Julian and Pomponius, this fragment is immediately followed by *lex* 48 from Paul saying that "nonetheless he is also liable under the action arising from a contract of partnership" and Paul continues in *lex* 50 "But he claims in terms of the action arising from partnership, as he ought to be content with one of these two actions because both look to the claiming of the article, not as in the case of the action for theft, only to punishment." In D. 9, 2, 18 Paul argues on the same hypothesis, although here no mention is made of the nature of the action. He says "but also if[16] he who received a slave as a pledge, killed him, or wounded him, he can be sued in terms of the *lex Aquilia* and the *actio pignoraticia*. But the plaintiff will have to be content with one or the other." Therefore here you have a new example of an internal contradiction in the Law of Justinian. Of course, I know that Schilter (the said *Exercitatio ad Pandectas*, 19, § 43) wants to reconcile Paul with Ulpian, namely on the grounds that Paul does not exclude the penalty. But in as much as that reconciliation seems to be based on the words of the said D. 17, 2, 50 "not as in the case of the action for theft, only to punishment", so again the other conjecture is the more cogent, namely that Paul in the said D. 17, 2, 50 and D. 9, 2, 18 considered the action under the *lex Aquilia* purely reipersecutory, for he stated that the action *ex contractu* and the action of the *lex Aquilia* extinguish one another. But if he had considered the action of the *lex Aquilia* as mixed, he would have said that the *actio pro socio* or the *actio pignoraticia* would extinguish the action from the *lex Aquilia*, except in as far as the latter is more extensive and includes a penalty as well. But even if we were to concede that Paul considered the action of the *lex Aquilia* as mixed (which however does not appear to be the case from what is said) a contradiction would nevertheless remain, because that Ulpian considers it purely penal, as said above, and this will become clearer from what follows.

---

[16] D. 9, 2, 18 reads *et si*, not *etsi*.

§. XXIV.

Quæritur enim, an actio L. Aquiliæ in heredes detur? Si Paulus respondere debuisset, respondisset haud dubio dari, cum sit rei persecutoria. Imperator vero JUSTINIANUS respondit in *f. 9. Inst. b. t.* eam contra heredes non dari, cum sit pœnalis. *Conf. supra f. 22.* Eaque in re iterum secutus est ULPIANUM *l. 23. f. 8. b. t. Hanc actionem & heredi ceterisque succefforibus dari conftat, fed in heredem vel cæteros hæc actio non dabitur, cum fit pænalis; nifi forte ex damno locupletior heres factus fit.* Quodfi enim Ulpianus pro mixta habuiffet, non dixiffet; cum fit pœnalis, fed: cum pœnam quoque contineat, vel quid fimile.

§. XXV.

Clarius id patet ex quæftione altera, quomodo plures teneantur, qui damnum dederunt, & an videlicet unius folutione liberentur reliqui. Tractat eam ULPIANUS *l. 11. f. 2. b. t. Sed fi plures fervum percufferint: utrum omnes, quafi occiderint, teneantur, videamus: & fi quidem apparet, cujus ictu perierit ille, quafi occiderit, tenetur. Quodfi non apparet; omnes, quafi occiderint, teneri, Julianus ait. Et fi cum uno agatur, cæteri non liberantur. Nam ex Lege Aquilia, quod alius præftitit, alium non relevat, cum fit pæna.* Si habuiffet pro mixta actione ineft pœna. Paulus ex fua hypothefi contra refpondiffet, unius folutione reliquos liberari, cum actio legis Aquiliæ rei perfecutionem contineat.

§. XXVI.

Venio ad quæftionem de furiofo damnum dante. Eum Jure Gentium teneri ad reparationem damni, fupra probavimus *f. 9.* Contra ULPIANUS, poftquam *l. 5. f. 1. b. t.* monuiffet *per damnum injuria datum bic intelligi, quod*

non

§ XXIV

Now there is the question whether the action of the *lex Aquilia* is granted against heirs. If Paul had been obliged to reply, he would without doubt have said that it is granted, since it is reipersecutory. But the Emperor Justinian in *Inst.* 4, 3, 9 replied that it is not granted against heirs since it is penal. Compare § 22 above. And on this matter he again follows Ulpian (D. 9, 2, 23, 8):

> It is agreed that this action is also granted to an heir and to other successors but this action will not be granted against an heir or other successors, since it is penal; unless by chance the heir has been enriched because of the damage done.

Now if Ulpian had considered it mixed he would not have said "since it is penal", but he would have said "since it also contains a penalty" or something similar.

§ XXV

This becomes clearer from the second question, i.e. how several people who did the damage are liable and whether indeed if one pays, the others are released from liability. Ulpian treats of this in D. 9, 2, 11, 2 where he says,

> But if several persons have struck and killed a slave, let us see whether all are liable for killing and if indeed it is apparent from whose blow the slave died, then that man is liable for the killing. But if it is not apparent, Julian says that all are liable as if they had all killed and if the action is brought against any one of them the others are not released from liability. For in terms of the *lex Aquilia* what one man pays does not release another, since the law is penal.

But if he had considered it mixed, there is a penalty element present. Paul on his hypothesis would have replied the opposite, namely that if one pays the others are released, since the action of the *lex Aquilia* involves the claiming of a thing.

§ XXVI

I come now to the question of a madman doing damage. I have proved above, § 9, that, in terms of the *Ius Gentium*, he is liable for making good the damage. On the other hand, Ulpian, after he advised in D. 9, 2, 5, 1 that "by damage done unlawfully is here understood that which

non jure factum est, i.e. dolo vel culpa *damum* ; subjungit *§.2. Et ideo quærimus, si furiosus damnum dederit, an legis Aquiliæ actio sit, & Pegasus negavit. Quæ enim in eo culpa sit, cum suæ mentis non sit? & hoc verissimum. Cessabit igitur Aquilia actio. Quemadmodum si quadrupes damnum dederit, Aquilia cessat: aut si tegula ceciderit, sed & si infans damnum dederit, idem erit dicendum. Quodsi impubes id fecerit, Labeo ait, quia furti tenetur, teneri & Aquiliæ eum. Et puto verum, si sit jam injuriæ capax.*

§. XXVII.

Quod vero rationem Ulpiani attinet, ideo non dari in furiosum Legis Aquiliæ actionem, quod furiosus nec doli, nec culpæ sit capax, ea ex supra dictis impugnari potest. Si enim damnum injuria datum, est damnum, quod non jure sit, non videtur furiosus aut infans liberari ab actione legis Aquiliæ, quia & damnum ab his datum non sit jure: nullum enim jus habent furiosus aut infans damnum dandi. Melius itaque fecisset Ulpianus, si & hic hypothesin suam sequens dixisset, quia actio Legis Aquiliæ pœnalis est. Pœna enim haud dubie non cadit in furiosum & infantem.

§. XXVIII.

Illustrantur dicta exinde, quod ULPIANUS *d.l.5. §.2.* furiosum & infantem damnum dantes comparet cum damno a quadrupedibus dato, ubi etiam cesset actio L. Aquiliæ. Quodsi enim habuisset actionem Legis Aquiliæ pro rei persecutoria vel mixta, non valeret multum hæc comparatio, quia ob damnum a quadrupede datum datur peculiaris actio rei persecutoria *t.t. si quadrupes.* Deberet ergo similiter dari actio aliqua de damno vel si mavis, pauperie a furioso datis. Sed cum actio L. Aquiliæ pro pœnali fuerit

C 3   habita,

has been done without right", i.e. done by intent or negligence, adds in D. 9, 2, 5, 2:

> And therefore we ask whether there is an action in terms of the *lex Aquilia* when a madman has done damage. Pegasus thinks not. For what fault is there in one who is out of his mind? This is very true. Therefore the action of the *lex Aquilia* will fail. Just as it fails when a four-footed beast has done damage, or a tile has fallen. Also, the same will have to be said if an infant has done damage. But if one under the age of puberty did it, Labeo says that, because[17] he is liable for theft, he is also liable for the action of the *lex Aquilia*. And I think this is sound, if he is already able to distinguish between right and wrong.

§ XXVII

As far as concerns Ulpian's reasoning that the action of the *lex Aquilia* is not granted against a madman, because a madman is capable neither of intent nor negligence, this can be countered by what was said above. For if damage has been unlawfully done, it is damage which is done without right, and it does not seem that a madman or an infant is released from the action of the *lex Aquilia*, because the damage done by them is done without right. For a madman or an infant has no right to do damage. Therefore Ulpian would have done better if here too, following his own hypothesis, he had said that the reason is because the action of the *lex Aquilia* is penal. For a penalty without doubt does not fall on a madman or an infant.

§ XXVIII

What has been said is elucidated by the fact that Ulpian in the said D. 9, 2, 5, 2 compares a madman and an infant doing damage with damage done by four-footed beasts, for there too the action under the *lex Aquilia* fails. But if he had considered the action of the *lex Aquilia* as reipersecutory or mixed, this comparison would not have much validity, because for damage done by a four-footed beast a specific reipersecutory action is given (the whole of D. 9, 1). Therefore some action for damage or if you prefer it for *pauperies* done by a madman should have been granted on the same lines. But since the action of the *lex Aquilia* has been considered

---

[17] Reading *quia* not *qui* as in the 1703 edition.

habita, actio vero, si quadrupes pauperiem fecisse dicatur
ad furiosum non quadret, (vide JOH. THOMÆ *de noxia ani-*
mal. cap. 2. num. 11. Illustr. Dn. STRYKE *in Usu mod. ad tit. si*
quadrupes ff. 1.) hinc non potuerunt interpretes Juris Roma-
mani salvis suis principiis ullam actionem hic concedere.
Dn. STRYKE *d. l. ff. 2.*

§. XXIX.

Quare & in eo abit a Jure Gentium actio Legis Aquiliæ, quod cum actio Juris Gentium de damno reparando non
ex delicto oriatur, sed ex æquitate *vid. ff. 10.* actio Legis A-
quiliæ ab interpretibus, qui eam pro pœnali habuerunt non
potuit non etiam pro actione ex delicto haberi. Idque diserte asserit JUSTINIANUS *pr. Instit. de Obl. quæ ex delicto*
nasc. secutus ea in re CAJUM *l. 4. de O. & A.*

§. XXX.

Denique id Juri Gentium superaddidit Lex Aquilia,
ut cum illo Jure perpetuo in simplum directa sit actio de re-
parandis damnis, lege Aquilia cautum fuerit, ut adversus
inficiantem in duplum actio detur, ULPIANUS *l. 2. ff. 1.* adversus confitentem in simplum. *Idem l. 23. ff. 10. hic.* Nihil tamen hic duri aut iniqui subest, uti in primaria disposi-
tione Legis Aquiliæ. Cum enim probatio damni dati sæpe
sit difficilis, metu hoc negantes, se damnum dedisse, reos
adigere voluit Lex Aquilia ad confessionem, ut actores hac
parte aliquo modo sublevaret.

§. XXXI.

Pergo ad Jus Canonicum. Etsi hoc non diserte quic-
quam abrogaverit & nominatim de actione Legis Aquiliæ,
sunt tamen quidam textus, ex quibus interpretes communiter formarunt propositiones, doctrinæ Juris Romani de
actio-

as penal, and the action where a four-footed beast is said to have done damage does not apply to a madman (see J Thoma, *de noxia animalium, cap.2, § 11.* and Stryk, *Usus Modernus Pandectarum,* D. 9, 1, 1) the commentators on Roman Law could not have granted any action while at the same time maintaining their principles intact (see Stryk, the said D. 9, 1, 2).

§ XXIX

And so the action under the *lex Aquilia* also deviates from the *Ius Gentium* in the respect that since the action of the *Ius Gentium* for making good damage does not arise from delict but from equity (see § 10 above) the action of the *lex Aquilia* could not but be regarded as an action *ex delicto* by the commentators who considered it penal. And Justinian asserts this specifically in *Inst.*4, 1, pr., following in this respect Gaius in D. 44, 7, 4.

§ XXX

In conclusion the *lex Aquilia* added to the *Ius Gentium* the proviso that although the direct action for making good damage by that universal law is for the simple value, it was laid down by the *lex Aquilia* that an action for double should be given against the defendant who denied the charge (Ulpian in D. 9, 2, 1) but for the simple value against one who admitted responsibility (Ulpian in D. 9, 2, 23, 10). Here, however, there is nothing harsh or inequitable, as in the basic provisions of the *lex Aquilia.* For since the proof of damage done is often difficult, the *lex Aquilia* wished to compel to a confession those who through fear deny that they did damage, so that it might thereby relieve plaintiffs of this aspect.

§ XXXI

I proceed to the Canon Law. Even although it did not distinctly and specifically abrogate anything regarding the action of the *lex Aquilia,* there are however certain texts from which the Commentators generally have formulated propositions contrary to the teaching of Roman Law on

actione Legis Aquiliæ contrarias. Videamus ipfos textus. Ex EUSEBIO PAPA refertur, *can. in legibus Cap. 12. quæft. 2.* quod res Ecclefiæ furripiens debeat cum pœna multiplicationis eam reftituere. *In legibus feculi,* inquit Papa, *cautum habetur (qui rem furripit alienam, illi, cujus res direpta eft, in undecuplum, quæ fublata funt, reftituat.) Et in lege divina legitur (maledictus omnis, qui transfert terminos proximi fui: & dicit omnis populus, Amen.) Talia ergo non præfumantur absque ultione, nec exerceantur absque fua damnatione. Proinde fi quis Ecclefiafticas oblationes, & quod DEO confecratum eft rapuerit, vel confenferit facientibus, ut facrilegus dijudicetur, & damnum in quadruplum reftituat, & canonice pæniteat.* Contra tamen fcripfit GREGORIUS *in canone ftatim fubfequente. Fraternitas tua ex perfona furis penfare poteft, qualiter valeat corrigi. Sunt enim quidam, qui habentes fubfidia furtum perpetrant: & funt alii, qui hac in re ex inopia delinquunt. Unde neceffe eft, ut quidam damnis, quidam vero verberibus & quidam diftrictius, quidam vero lenius corrigantur. Et cum paulo diftrictius agitur, ex charitate agendum eft, & non ex furore: quia ipfi hoc præftatur, qui corrigitur, ne gebennæ ignibus tradatur. Et infra. Addis etiam an pro augmento ea, quæ furto de Ecclefiis abftulerunt, reddere debeant. Sed abfit, ut Ecclefia cum augmento recipiat, quod de terrenis rebus videtur amittere; & lucra damnis quærat.* GRATIANUS, utpote, qui Concordiam difcordantium Canonum fcribere voluit, hæc duo fic conciliat, *quod illud Eufebii de Legum feveritate, illud Gregorii de Ecclefiaftica manfuetudine debeat intelligi.* Id certe conftat, Gregorium noluiffe, ab iis etiam, qui dolo malo damnum dederunt, plus repeti, quam veram damni reftitutionem.

§ XXXII.

the action of the *lex Aquilia.* Let us look at the actual texts. From Pope Eusebius (C. 12, q. 2, c. 10) is drawn the statement that someone stealing church property ought to restore it with a multiple penalty. The Pope says:

> In the laws of the world it is laid down that "he who steals someone else's property shall restore to him whose property was stolen up to eleven fold[18] what was stolen" and in Divine Law we read "Cursed be he that removeth his neighbour's landmarks and all the people say Amen" (Deuteronomy, 27. 17). Therefore such acts are not undertaken without vengeance, nor are they done without their appropriate punishment. Further if anyone seizes offerings made to the Church and that which has been consecrated to God, or conspires with those so doing, let him be adjudged a temple robber and let him restore what he has taken fourfold and do canonical penance.

On the other hand, Gregory, in the canon following immediately thereon (C. 12, q. 2, c. 11) has written:

> Brother, one can consider how a thief is best to be corrected from the character of the thief. For there are some who although they have means of support, commit theft and there are others who sin in this matter because of want. Hence it is necessary that some are corrected by fines, others by flogging and some more severely, others less so. And when a somewhat more severe punishment is meted out, it must be done in love and not in anger because this is done to him so that he who is corrected be not delivered into the fires of Hell.

And in the paragraph below:

> You also ask whether they ought to restore those things which they stole from Churches together with something more. But let it not be that the Church receives with increase what it appears to lose of its earthly possessions and that it should seek profit from damage.

Gratian indeed, who wished to a write a reconciliation of conflicting Canons, reconciles these two thus:

> That remark[19] of Eusebius' ought to be understood of the severity of the laws, that of Gregory of the mercy of the Church.

Certainly it is established that Gregory did not wish more than the true restitution of damage to be claimed even from those who did damage with malicious intent.

---

[18] Friedberg in his edition of the Corpus Iuris Canonici (1879 - 1881) gives as alternative readings *quadruplum* and *decuplum.*

[19] The Friedberg edition has *dictum.*

§. XXXII.

Affinis præcedenti eſt *canon. ſi Epiſcopum 3. C. 16. q̃. 6.* decerptus ex GREGORII epiſtolis. *Si Epiſcopum, inquit, talem culpam admiſiſſe conſtiterit (quod abſit) ut conſtet eum non irrationabiliter fuiſſe depoſitum, eadem ejus depoſitio confirmetur, & Eccleſiæ res ſuæ omnes reſtituantur, quæ ablatæ claruerint: quia delictum perſonæ in damnum Eccleſiæ non eſt convertendum. Si enim, ut dicunt, Comitiolus defunctus eſt, ab herede ejus, quæ injuſte ab illo ablata ſunt, ſine excuſatione reddantur.* Igitur Jure Canonico tenentur heredes etiam, defuncti damnum ab hoc datum reparare.

§. XXXIII.

Neque ſolum talia inculcentur in decreto, ſed & Epiſtolæ decretales idem ſentiunt. *Parochiano tuo, ita ſcripſit* GREGORIUS IX *cuidam Epiſcopo, cap. ult. X. de ſepulturis, qui excommunicatus pro manifeſtis exceſſibus, videlicet homicidio, incendio, violenta manuum injectione in perſonas Eccleſiaſticas, Eccleſiarum violatione vel inceſtu fuit, dum ageret in extremis, per Presbyterum ſuum juxta formam Eccleſiæ abſolutus, non debent cœmiterium & alia Eccleſiæ ſuffragia denegari. Sed ejus heredes & propinqui, ad quos bona pervenerunt ipſius, ut pro eodem ſatisfaciant, cenſura ſunt Eccleſiaſtica compellendi.*

§. XXXIV.

Non tamen tenentur heredes Jure Canonico ultra damnum datum, quid pœnæ loco ſolvere, ut qui ne quidem eo Jure tenentur ultra vires hereditatis. Ita enim reſcripſit ALEXANDER III. Claremontenſi Epiſcopo *cap. 5. X. de Raptoribus. In literis tuis continebatur, quod cum H. multis fuiſſet criminibus irretitus, qui Eccleſiarum incendium dia-*

bolo

§ XXXII

Canon C. 16, q. 6, c. 2(3), taken from the letters of Gregory, is related to the preceding. Gregory says:

> If it is established that a Bishop has committed such a crime (preserve us therefrom) and he clearly has not been deposed without reason, let his actual deposition be confirmed and let all the property which it is clear[20] has been taken away, be restored to the Church, because a sin committed by somebody ought not to redound to the detriment of the Church. If, however, as they say, your colleague has died, let those things which he unjustly took away, be returned without excuse by his heir.

Therefore by Canon Law, heirs are also liable to repay the damage done by the deceased.

§ XXXIII

Not only are such views strongly emphasised in the Decretum but decretal letters express the same view. For thus did Gregory IX write to a certain Bishop (X 3, 28, 14):

> With regard to that member of your congregation who had been excommunicated for manifest sins, namely for homicide, incendiarism, violent laying of hands on the persons of clerics, violation and defiling of Churches, and then when he was *in extremis*, was absolved by the parish priest according to ecclesiastical form, he ought not to be denied church burial and other rites of the Church. But his heirs and kinsmen to whom his property has come, are to be compelled by Ecclesiastical sanction to make satisfaction on his behalf.

§ XXXIV

However, by Canon Law heirs are not liable to pay anything by way of penalty, over and above the damage done, so that not even by that Law are they liable beyond the value of the inheritance. For thus did Alexander III write to the Bishop of Claremont (X 5, 17, 5),

> In your letter you wrote that when H. had been stirred up to many crimes, for with the prompting of the Devil

---

[20] The Friedberg edition reads *fuerant* for *claruerint*.

Ialo, instigante commiserat, tandem in ægritudine constitutus, accepta pænitentia de commissis, per manum capellani sui fuit a sententia anathematis absolutus: sed moriens Ecclesiasticam sepulturam habere nequivit. Quapropter si ita res se habet, mandamus, ut corpus ejusdem, adpell. cess. facias in cœmiterio sepeliri, & heredes ejus moneas & compellas, ut his, quibus ille per incendium, vel alio modo damna contra justitiam irrogaverat, juxta facultates suas condigne satisfaciant, ut sic a peccato valeat liberari.

§. XXXV.

Fateor quidem allegatos textus de actione damni ob culpam dati non specialiter loqui, sed ubique memorari homicidia, furta, rapinas, incendia: id tamen exinde generaliter a Doctoribus infertur: Jure Canonico heredes defuncti teneri ex delicto defuncti, quod Jure Civili secus erat. Malo recitare hic verba EMERICI de ROSBACH *de comparatione Juris Civilis & Canonici lib. 3. tit. 25. comp. 4. De Jure Civili,* inquit, *heres ex delicto defuncti non potest conveniri, neque tenetur, nisi quatenus ad eum ex delicto pervenit: vel nisi lis cum defuncto contestata sit,* l. post litis contestationem C. si ex delict. defunct. *De Jure vero Canonico heres ex maleficio defuncti, cujus bona percepit, licet ex maleficio ad eum nihil pervenit, tenetur,* c. si Episcopum 3. Caus. 16. qu. 6. & ibi glos. in verb. reddantur, c. tua nos, de usur. c. ult. de Sepult. c. in literis, de raptor. *Ratio, quia delictum personæ in*   '   *   non debet,* text. in d. l. si episcopum, & *ut defunctus per restitutionem damni dati a peccato valeat liberari,* text. in d. c. in literis in fin. *Non tamen heredes ultra facultates vel vires hereditatis defuncti malefactoris tenentur,* text. & gloss. in d. c. in literis, *si inventarium fecerint,*

D   *rint,*

he had set alight Churches, nevertheless during his last illness, having done penance for his sins, he was absolved from the sentence of excommunication by his chaplain but on dying he was not able to have Ecclesiastical burial. Wherefore, if the position is as you say, we give orders that, the previous decision being void, you see to the burial of his body in the cemetery and you warn and compel his heirs that, according to their means, they should properly give satisfaction to those on whom he unlawfully inflicted damage by arson or in any other way, so that thus he may be freed from sin.

§ XXXV

Indeed, I admit that the texts cited are not speaking specifically about the action for damage done through fault, but everywhere they mention homicide, theft, robbery and arson. However, from this it is inferred generally by the learned commentators that in Canon Law the heirs of the deceased are liable for the delict of the deceased. This was not the case in the Civil Law. Here I like to quote the words of Emericus de Rosbach *Comparatio Iuris Civilis et Canonici*, 3. 25. 4). He says:

In the Civil Law an heir cannot be sued for the delict of the deceased, nor is he liable except in as far as he was enriched by the delict, or unless suit has already been joined with the deceased (C. 4, 17, 1) but in the Canon Law an heir is liable for the offence of the deceased whose property he has inherited even though nothing has accrued to him from the offence (C. 16, q. 6, c. 2(3) and the gloss there on the word *reddantur;* X.5, 19, 9; X.3, 28, 14; X.5, 17, 5). The reason being that a man's sins ought not to redound to the detriment of the Church (see the said C. 16, q. 6, c. 2(3)) and that the deceased can only be freed from sin by the restitution of the damage done (see the said X 5, 17, 5). However, the heirs are not liable beyond the means and assets of the inheritance of the deceased malefactor (see the text of X 5, 7, 5 and the gloss thereon) provided they have made an inventory

rint, ut dicis Gloss. in d. c. in literis in verb. *juxta facultates*, per l. Sancimus, §. fin autem, & §. seq. C. de jure deliberandi.

§. XXXVI.

Quodsi igitur æquitas Juris Canonici heredes defuncti voluit teneri ad restitutionem damni, quod dolo malo defuncti datum est ; de quo major erat dubitandi ratio, multo magis tenebuntur ad resarcitionem, si non ex delicto vero teneatur defunctus, sed ex mera æquitate, veluti si culpa, etiam levissima damnum dederit: unde hanc dispositionem Juris Canonici non insulse ad Legis Aquiliæ actionem Romanam applicuit CYPRIANUS REGNERUS *in censura Belgica ad institutiones h. t. §.9.*

§. XXXVII.

Miror adeo, quod Clarissimus BOEKELMANNUS *in differentiis Juris Civilis & Canonici Cap.44.* asseruerit, in doctrina de damno injuria dato nullam occurrere differentiam alicujus momenti, cum tamen hactenus dicta contrarium ostendant. Miror etiam, cur *in cap. seq. 45. n. 2.* scripserit: *Jure Canonico actio injuriarum datur heredi & in heredem* c. in literis § X. de rapt. *Ratio: quia Jus Canonicum credit animas defunctorum puniri in Purgatorio, donec pro peccato satisfiat.* Etenim Jus Canonicum in *d. Cap. 5.* plane de actione injuriarum quanta quanta est, non sit rei persecutoria, sed pure poenalis & meram vindictam sapiat, textus vero adductus Juris Canonici loquatur de actionibus rei persecutoriis.

§. XXXVIII.

Mores Germaniæ quod concernit, ante omnia separandi sunt mores antiqui a novioribus. Illos, quod attinet, proli-

as the Glossator says in the said X.5, 17, 5 on the words *juxta facultates.*

§ XXXVI

But if, therefore, the equity of Canon Law wished the heirs of the deceased to be liable for restitution of damage which was done through the malicious intent of the deceased, a proposition where there was considerable reason for doubt, how much more will they be liable for making good if the deceased was indeed not liable in delict but on the grounds of pure equity, e.g. if he did damage through negligence, even very slight negligence. Hence Cyprianus Regneris in *Censura Belgica, ad Inst.*4, 3, 9 wisely applies this provision of Canon Law to the Roman action of the *lex Aquilia.*

§ XXXVII

I am surprised that the most distinguished Boekelmann in his *De Differentiis Juris Civilis et Canonici, cap.* 44 averred that in the theory about damage done unlawfully no discrepancy of any significance occurs, although what has been said thus far points out a contradiction. I also wonder why in the following chapter, 45. 2, he wrote:

> In the Canon Law the *actio iniuriarum* is granted to an heir and against an heir (X.5, 17, 5). The reason is that the Canon Law believes that the souls of the deceased are punished in Purgatory until satisfaction is done for sin.

Now the Canon Law in the said chapter 5 is clearly sensible to the fact that the *actio iniuriarum,* such as it is, is not reipersecutory but simply penal and looks to pure vengeance, but the text cited from the Canon Law speaks about reipersecutory actions.

§ XXXVIII

As far as concerns the customs of Germany, first and foremost the ancient customs must be distinguished from the more recent. With regard to the former

prolixi hic esse nolumus, cum eos satis jam exposuerit Cele-
berrimus SCHILTERUS *Exerc. ad Pand. XIX. th. 52. 53. 54. 55.*
ubi potissimas Leges Wisigothorum, Burgundionum, Ale-
mannorum, Baivariorum, Ripuariorum, Saxonum, Friso-
num, Longobardorum huc pertinentes excerpsit, ex quibus omnibus patet, regulariter ab omnibus hisce populis
petitam fuisse simplicem rei aestimationem , addita saltem
quandoque poena, eaque legibus determinata, si dolo damnum quis dederit; quod plane abit a natura actionis Legis Aquiliae.

§. XXXIX.

Videamus paulo distinctius mores Germanorum pau-
lulum propiores temporibus nostris, quos non melius poterimus cognoscere, quam ex speculis Juris Suevici & Saxonici, utpote in quibus collecti sunt mores totius Juris Germanici. Ex speculo Suevico huc pertinet Landr. *cap. 228.*
(Sec Edit. Goldasti in Reichs-Satungen. Und ist, daß ein
Mann ein Baum zu Wald hauet dem Weg so nahen, daß er
uff den Weg fallen mag, schlecht der Baum ein Menschen zu
tod, man soll ihm das Haupt abschlahen; schlecht er ein Vieh
zu tod, er soll es gelten als es werth was, und dem Richter wet-
ten ein Fräffel. Item *cap. 233.* Ein jeglich Mann soll gelten
den Schaden, der von seinen Schulden geschicht mit geschicht,
(SCHILTERUS *d. Exerc. 19. s. 56.* notat legendum mit Ge-
schihte i. e. Geschütte cum projectu terrae, cum fontes & fo-
veae effodiuntur aut cellae.) Der Brunnen oder Gruben
gräbet, der soll sie bewahren und verbrücken, als hoch ob der
Erden, daß es einen Mann gang über sein Knie. Thut er das
nicht, was Schaden darvon geschicht, den soll er gelten. Wer
ein Keller oder ein andere Grub grabet, der soll sie ohn ander

Leut

we do not intend to be prolix here since the celebrated Schilter has already expounded them adequately (*Exercitationes ad Pandectas*, 19, §§ 52-55). There he excerpted especially the Laws of the Visigoths, the Burgundians, the Allemanni, the Baivarii, the Ripuarian Franks, the Saxons, the Frisians and the Lombards which pertain to this question and from all these it is clear that as a rule the simple value of the article was claimed by all these people. A penalty was sometimes added and that was determined by law, if someone did damage maliciously. This clearly is far from the nature of the action of the *lex Aquilia*.

§ XXXIX

Let us consider somewhat more carefully the customs of the Germans a little closer to our own times. We can become acquainted with these no better than from the *Schwabenspiegel* and the *Sachenspiegel* since herein are collected all the customary laws of the Germans. From the *Schwabenspiegel* to the matter in hand pertains *Landrecht, cap.* 228 (according to the edition of Goldast in the Imperial Statues):

And if someone cuts a tree in the forest, but so close to a road that it may fall on to it, one shall decapitate him, if a person is killed by the tree; if it is a head of cattle that is killed, he has to pay its value as compensation and promise a penalty to the judge.

Likewise *cap.* 233[21]:

Everybody has to make good the damage that occurs through his fault '*mit geschicht*' (Schilter, the said *Exercitationes* 19. § 57[22] observes that this is to be read '*mit Geschütte*', i.e. on mounds of earth when wells or pits or cellars are being dug.) Whoever digs wells or holes has to guard and fence them as high off the ground as the knee of a man. If he fails to do this, he is liable for the damage arising. Whoever digs a cellar or another hole has to do this without causing damage to other

---

[21] Schilter cites this as Landrecht I 189.

[22] Not 56 but 57.

Leut Schaden machen, und soll sie nicht fürbaß in die Straffe setzen, wann sie den Schuh. Item *cap. 354.* Und hat ein Mann ein schlahendes Pferd, und wußt er das wol. Wann er drauf sitz, so soll er die Leut von ihm heissen gan, und soll von den Leuten reuten. Und thut er das nicht, welchen Schaden es thut, er soll ihn gelten. Thut aber er, als hievor gesprochen ist, so giltet er nicht. Porro *cap. 363. 364.* Wer einen Leythund stilt oder zu tod schlecht, der soll seinem Herren des der Hund was, einen andern als guten geben, als jener was, und soll ihm sechs Schilling darzu geben. Wer einen Hund stilet, der ein Treibhund heisset, er soll dem Herren als gutten wieder geben und drey Schilling darzu. Sequente *cap. 365.* idem disponitur, si quis occidat einen Spürhund, Byberhund, Windhund, Wachtelhund rc. nisi quod pro singulis h sce generibus pœne variet. Tum sequitur in *cap. 366.* Und ist daß ein Hund einen Mann anlauffet und ihm in sein Gewand beisset, oder in sein bloße Haut, wo das an seinem Lybe ist, und wehret er sich, und schlecht ihm zu todte, er soll Ihm einen als guten wieder geben, als jener was, und einen Pfenning und nicht mehr. Es soll aber jener, deß der Hund was, jenen seinen Schaden halber obliegen, oder er soll ihm des Hundes nicht gelten, und soll auch dem Richter nit büssen. Item *cap. 367.* Und ist, daß ein Mann einen Hund wundet, daß er lahm wird an den Beinen, und ist niemand nütze, so soll er ihm haben den lamen Hund und soll jenen einen als guten Hund wieder geben, als jener was, und viel Pfenning darzu, als davor geschrieben ist. Confer & *cap. 368. 369.* quæ disponunt de Accipitribus & Falconibus furto ablatis & occisis simili modo.

§. LX.

Ex Speculo Saxonico ejusque jure provinciali huc
pertl.

people, and he must not put them further into the road than seven feet.
Likewise *cap.* 354:

And if a man has a horse that kicks, and he knows about it, when he rides it, he shall tell the people to go away from him and he shall ride away from them. And if he does not do so, he shall be liable for the damage done by the horse. If, however, he does what has been set out above, he is not liable.

Likewise *cap.* 363, 364:

Whoever steals or kills a lead dog shall give its owner another lead dog of the same quality, and he shall give him six *schillings* over and above. Whoever steals a dog that is referred to as '*Treibhund*' (hunting dog) has to give its owner another dog of the same quality plus three *schillings.*

The following *cap.* 365 lays down the same:

If someone kills a tracker dog, a beaver hound, a greyhound or a quaildog, it is only the penalty that varies with regard to the individual breeds.

Cap. 366 follows with:

And if a dog jumps at someone and bites the clothes he is wearing, or his bare skin, in whichever part of his body, and if that person defends himself and kills the dog, he has to give him a dog of the same quality plus one *pfennig* and not more. But the other who owned the dog is liable to make good the damage done to the other person, or he shall not claim on account of the dog and shall also not be liable to the judge.

Likewise *cap.* 367:

And if someone injures a dog in such a way that it becomes lame and is no longer of any use, he may keep the lame dog and shall give the owner a dog of the same quality as he had plus as many *pfennigs* as is provided in this case.

Compare also *cap.* 368, 369 which deal in a similar manner with stealing and killing falcons and sparrow hawks.

§ XL[23]

From the *Sachenspiegel* and its provincial law to the matter in hand

---

[23] Reading *XL* for *LX* as in the 1703 edition.

pertinent *lib. 2. art. 38.* Der Mann soll gelten den Schaden, der von seiner Verwahrlosung wegen andern Leuten geschiehet, es sey von Feuer oder Wasser (Brunnen) das er nicht bewirkt hat eines Knies hoch über der Erden. *Art. 39.* Welch wegfärtiger Mann Korne auf dem Felde fretzet, und den mit sich nirgend hinführet, der gilt den Schaden auch seinen Würden. *Lib. 2. art. 46.* Wer besäet Land eines andern Mannes anderweit eeret, der soll Ihm den Schaden gelten als recht ist, und Ihm darzu sein Buß geben. *Art. 47.* Wer sein Vieh auf eines andern Mannes Korn treibet, oder auf sein Graß, der soll ihm gelten den Schaden auf recht und darzu die That verbüssen mit dreyen Schillingen. *Art. 48.* Lesset ein Mann sein Korn draussen stehen, als andre Leut ihr Korn ein haben geführet, wird es ihm gefretzet oder abgetreten, man gilt es ihm nicht. *Art. 62.* Schlegt ein Mann einen Hund zu todt, oder einen Beeren, oder ein ander Thier, indem als es ihm Schaden will thun, er bleibet es ohne Schaden, ob er das schweren thar auff den Heiligen, daß er es in Nothwer thete, und Ihm anders nicht steuren kunte. Ex *libro 3. art. 48.* Wer des andern Vieh tödtet, also das mans doch essen mag, mit willen oder unwillen, der muß es gelten mit seinem gesatzten Wehrgeld. Lehmet er es aber, er gilt es mit seinem halben Wehrgeld ohne Buß. Darzu behelt jener sein Viehe auch, deß es vor was. Wer aber tödtet oder lehmet an einen Fuß ein Viehe gerne, oder ohne Noth, daß man es nicht essen mag, es soll es gelten mit vollem Wehrgeld, und auch mit Buß. Lehmet er es aber an einem Aug, er gilt es mit dem halben Theil. Bleibet aber ein Viehe todt oder lahm von eines Mannes Schuld und ohn seinen Willen, und thut er seinen Eyd darzu, er bleibet es ohne Buß, als hievor geredt ist. Lehmet aber ein Mann einen Hund

und

pertains *lib. 2, art.* 38:

> A man shall make good any damage that he has done to others through his negligence: whether he has caused it by way of a fire or as a result of failing to fence in a well to the height of the knee above the ground.

Book 2, Art. 39:

> Every traveller who eats corn in the field, without however taking it anywhere, has to make good the damage according to the value.

Book 2, Art. 46:

> Whoever ploughs up someone else's land that has been sown has to make good such damage as is right, and in addition he shall pay him a penalty.

Book 2, Art. 47:

> Whoever drives his cattle on to the cornfield or on to the meadow of another has to make good the damage as the law provides and in addition he shall be fined three *schillings* for his act.

Book 2, Art. 48:

> If someone leaves his crop unharvested when other people have already brought theirs in, and then it gets eaten up or trampled down, no compensation is due.

Book 2, Art. 62:

> If someone kills a dog or a bear or another animal because it attacked him, he remains without penalty, provided he swears by the saints that he acted in self-defence and could not deal with the matter differently.

From Book 3, Art. 48:

> If someone, whether intentionally or unintentionally, kills another's beast but in such a way that one may still eat it, he has to pay for it the statutory blood-money (*Wergeld*). If he injures it, he has to pay for it with half of the blood-money and without penalty. Apart from that he to whom the beast belonged retains it. But if someone intentionally and not in self-defence kills a beast, or injures it in the foot in such a way that one can no longer eat it, he has to make up for it by paying the full blood-money and also a penalty. If, however, he injures it in one of its eyes, he has to pay half. But if a beast is killed or injured through a man's fault - though not through his intention - provided he swear an oath, he does not have to pay penalty, as has been said previously. But if someone injures

und schlegt ihn zu todt, so er ihn beissen will, oder sein Vieh auf der Strassen, oder auf dem Felde, er bleibt es ohne Wandel, geweret er es auf den Heiligen, daß er ihm anders nicht gesteuren kunte. *Art. 49.* Welch Hund zu Felde gehet, den soll man an Band halten, durch daß er niemand schade. Thut er aber Schaden, den soll er gelten, dem der Hund folget zu Felde, oder sein Herr, ob er selber, der ihn führet, des nicht gelten mag.

§. XLI.

Jam quemadmodum aliunde conftat, & expreffe dicitur in Schwaben-Spiegel Landr. *cap. 393.* quod Jus Suevicum & Saxonicum non differant nifi in materia fuccedendi ab inteftato, & in proceffu ac modo fententias dandi, quia videlicet utrumque collectum eft ex moribus populi Germanici; ita apparebit etiam cuilibet, qui conferet excerpta Juris & Suevici & Saxonici hactenus recenfita, quod unum jus conveniat cum altero in eandem fententiam in doctrina de damno dato refarciendo, & quod unum facile ex altero declarari, aut ampliari, aut limitari poffit. Simul vere patebit, quod Germani in actione de damno dato refarciendo nunquam refpexerint ad formam Legis Aquiliæ, ut pœnæ loco aliquid repetierint, multo minus ut effentiale illud Legis Aquiliæ quanti res retro plurimi fuerit, obfervaverint. Sed regulariter data fuit actio de damno dato ad fimplicem reparationem damni. Vide excerpta ex Jure Suevico *cap. 233. 354.* Ex Jure Saxonico *lib. 2. art. 38. 39.* Quodfi tamen talia facta fint, quæ plerumque cum dolo malo fiunt, tunc præter damni reftitutionem folvere etiam debet damnum dans emendam Domino, nifi pecus interfectum comedi poffit, tunc enim faltem pretium folvit, fed Dominus pecudis

inter-

or kills a dog because it was about to bite him or his cattle, either on the road or in the field, he remains without penalty, provided he swears by the saints that he could not beat the dog back in any other way.

Book 3, Art. 49:

If one takes a dog into the country, one has to keep it on the lead, so that it may not injure anyone. But if the dog causes damage, it has to be paid for by the person whom the dog followed into the country; or by his master, if he whom he followed is not able to pay.

§ XLI

Now in as much as it is established from other sources and is expressly stated in the *Schwabenspiegel, Landrecht, cap.* 393 that the Law of the Suebi and the Law of the Saxons do not differ except with regard to succession *ab intestato* and in the process and method of passing sentence, because, of course, both are drawn from the customs of the German people, so also it will be clear to anyone who compares the excerpts from Suebian and Saxon Law cited thus far that they agree one with the other regarding the doctrine of making good damage done and that the one can easily be pronounced or extended with reference to the other. At the same time it will truly be clear that the Germans in the action for making good damage done never looked to the form of the *lex Aquilia* in order to claim something by way of a penalty, much less in order to adopt the very essence of the *lex Aquilia*, namely the requirement 'of the highest value of the property retrospectively'. But as a rule the action for damage done was given for the simple reparation of the damage. See the excerpts from the Suebian Law, *cap.* 233 and 354, and from the Saxon Law, book 2, *art.* 38 and 39. But if, however, the damage done is such as is generally done with malicious intent, then in addition to the restitution of damage, the offender has to pay the owner, in addition to the restitution of the damage, a further payment as amends, unless the animal killed can be eaten, for then he only pays the price while the owner of the slaughtered animal

interfectæ illam retinet. Quodfi dubium fit, utrum data opera damnum datum fit, tum reus cogitur fe purgare juramento & tum liberatur ab emenda. Vide reliquos articulos f. 39. & 40. excerptos. Igitur ut paucis totam rem exprimam. Culpa damnum dantis non coërcetur pœna: Dolus coërcetur quidem, fed pœna certa ac determinata, non incerta, uti in L. Aquilia.

§. XLII.

Unde facile patet, quid fentiendum fit de Philofophia celeberr. SCHILTERI *d. Exerc. XIX. f. 59. Atque adeo videtur,* inquit, *actionem damni fola culpa feu negligentia dati perfecutoriam, non effe pœnalem jure noftro: quippe cum nec pœna debeatur, nec quanti maximi valuerit.* ZOBEL. diff. l. C. & S. p. IV. diff. IX. & X. SCHNEIDEW. J. h. t §. penult. fin. STRUV. h. t. th. 25. *Ita & fentit* a LEUWEN Cenf. for. l. V. cap. 21. §. 16. *Verum cum non infpiciendum fit, quid tandem in fententiam venire poffit, fed quid in libellum: porro cum juramentum requiratur, quo culpa a dolo & proærefi purgetur,* d. art. 48. *adeoque cum dolus a culpa abeffe non præfumatur, fed juramento demum dolus a culpa feparetur: igitur regulariter præter damni æftimationem, etiam emenda feu pœna læfo debita peti poteft, atque ita pœnalem eam effe etiam noftro jure recte afferitur, neque adverfus heredes competere.* CARPZOV. 4 12. def. 9. H PISTOR. p. 1. qu. 27. RICHTER. dec. 35. 19.

§. XLIII.

Scilicet, uti de illa quæftione, an actio de damno dato moribus Germanorum in heredes tranfeat, infra fuo loco videbimus, ita funt, quæ in hac difputatione Schilteri, notam merentur, qua evincere vult, actionem de damno

dato

keeps the carcass. But if there is doubt whether the damage was done deliberately, then the accused is compelled to take a purgatory oath upon which he is released from making amends. See the other paragraphs quoted, §§39 and 40. Therefore to summarise the whole matter in a few words. Negligence on the part of the man doing damage is not punished. Intent is indeed punished but with a fixed and predetermined penalty not with an indefinite penalty as in the *lex Aquilia*.

§ XLII

Hence it is readily apparent what must be thought of the doctrine of the most eminent Schilter (the said *Exercitationes ad Pandectas*, 19. § 59). He writes:

> And so it seems that the action for damage done by mere *culpa*, that is by negligence, is, in our law, reipersecutory not penal, since, of course, no penalty is due nor is the property assessed at its greatest value. Zobellus, *Differentiae juris, part.* 4, *diff.* 9 *et* 10; Schneidewinus, *Ad Inst.* 4, 3 § *capite tertio*, 9; Struvius, *Evolutiones controversiarum*, D. 9, 2, *th.* 25. Van Leeuwen in *Censura Forensis* (*part.* 1, book V, *cap.* 21, § 16) says the same. But since one must not consider what can come into the sentence but what comes into statement of claim and further-more since an oath is required in order that the negligence be cleared of intent and forethought (the said art. 48) and indeed since intent is not presumed to be absent from negligence, but is only separated from negligence by the oath, therefore regularly an amends, that is a penalty owed to the injured party, can also be claimed, and so it is rightly asserted that, in our law too, this action is penal and is not available to heirs. See Carpzovius, *Jurisprudentia Forensis, part.* 4, *const.* XII, *def.* 9; Hartmann Pistoris, *Quaestiones, part.* I, *qu.* 27; Richter, *Decisiones juris, dec.* 55, 19.

§ XLIII

Now in as much as we shall deal below in the appropriate place with the question whether according to German custom the action for damages transmits to the heirs, so there are certain points in this discussion of Schilter's which deserve note. Here he wished to prove that the action for damage

dato pœnstem esse. Eñ; qdod in natura actionis determinanda non tam videndum sit, quid in sententiam veniat, quam quid in libellum, dicta tamen a nobis *f. 41.* satis ostendunt, in actione de damno dato regulariter peti saltem restitutionem damni. Fallitur vero SCHILTERUS, dum putat, *regulariter praeter* damni aestimationem etiam pœnam peti posse laeso debitam: Fallitur, dum putat, quod per *d. art. 48. lib. 3.* Landt. *regulariter* requiratur juramentum, quo culpa a dolo & proaeresi purgetur; Fallitur, dum putat, quod *regulariter* non praesumatur dolus a culpa abesse, sed quod juramento demum dolus a culpa separetur. Nam ut *d. f. 41.* dictum, citatus *art. 48.* continet exceptionem a regula non regulam ipsam. Intuitu igitur exceptionis actio de damno dato apud Germanos erat partim rei persecutoria, partim pœnalis. Sed quicquid tamen in hac actione pœnale erat, id toto cœlo differt ab omnibus actionibus pœnalibus Romanorum, ut latius ostendit Dn PRÆSES *in Differt. de Usu actionum pœnalium in foris Germaniae integro cap. 2.*

§. XLVI.

Videamus nunc mores hodiernos Germaniae. Licebit autem hos sistere verbis ILLUSTR ORDINARII NOSTRI *in Usu mod. Pand. ad tit. L. Aquil. f. 2. Quod usum fori attinet, communiter a Dd. approbata est sententia, hodie damnum non amplius aestimari secundum bonitatem in qua res antea fuit, sed secundum statum praesentem, in quo fuit tempore damni dati, ut hinc qui equum claudum occiderit, qui ante paucas septimanas pretiosissimus fuit, non nisi leve boc pretium, quo claudus ille equus vendi possit, refundere teneatur.* GRÖNWEGEN *de LL. abrog. ad f. 15. Instit. h. t.* CY-PRIAN.

done is penal. His argument is like this. Because in determining the nature of an action one must consider not only what comes into the sentence but also what comes into the statement of claim, my remarks in § 41 adequately show that in the action for damage done the claim is regularly only for restitution of damage. Therefore Schilter is wrong when he considers that *regularly* in addition to the evaluation of the damage done, a penalty owed to the injured party can also be claimed. He is wrong when he considers that by the said *art.* 48 of book 3 of the *Landrecht,* there is *regularly* the requirement for an oath whereby negligence is clear of intent and forethought. He is wrong when he considers that *regularly* intent is not presumed absent from negligence but that intent is only separated from negligence by an oath. For as was stated in the said § 41, *art.* 48 as cited contains an exception to the rule not the rule itself. Therefore in view of this exception the action for damage done was among the Germans partly reipersecutory and partly penal. But whatever the penal element in this action, it was entirely different from any penal action among the Romans, as I have shown extensively in my *Dissertatio,* the whole of Chapter 2.

§ XLIV

Let us now look at the present day customs of the Germans. I may base these on the words of our illustrious Professor (Stryk) in his *Usus Modernus Pandectarum ad* D. 9, 2, § 2. He says:

As pertains to legal practice, the view is generally approved by the learned authorities that today damage is no longer estimated according to the value which the thing had previously but with regard to the present state it was in at the time of the damage done. Thus he who killed a lame horse which a few weeks before was very valuable, is only liable to repay the trifling amount for which that lame horse could be sold. See Groenewegen in *De Legibus Abrogatis, ad Inst.* 4, 3, 15; Cyprianus [33]

PRIAN. REGNER *Censura Belgic. ad L. 2. pr. h. t.* ANTHON. MATTH *ad lib. 47. ff. tit. 3. cap. 3. num. 4.* STRUV. *h. t. 25.* SCHNEIDEWIN *ad ſ. 13. Inſt. h. t.* BRUNNEM. *ad L. 27. n. 7. h. t.* GIESEBERT *Juſtinian. Harm. v. t. n. 53. ubi hos mores univerſales dicit.*

§. XLV.

Digna quoque ſunt, quæ huc integre apponantur verba ſequentis *ſ. 3. Cum itaque Germani quondam ſoli damni præſentis reparatione fuerint contenti; hoc tantum quoad praxin remanet dubium, an recepto jure Romano a ſimplicitate priſtina in æſtimando damno diſceſſerint, & diverſam ejus conſiderationem ad ductum legis Aquiliæ receperint? Aſſerere hoc non auſim, cum recepto Jure Romano, priſtinæ Germanorum conſuetudines non penitus ſublatæ, ut hinc exiſtimem, in quo loco doceri non poteſt L. Aquiliam hoc intuitu ſpeciatim probatam eſſe, ibi damnum retro æſtimandum non eſſe. Locum autem, ubi L. Aquiliæ diſtincta æſtimatio in ſpecie approbata, nobis exhibet Boruſſia Electoralis, ubi libro 6 tit. 10. artic. 1 §. 5. ita cautum deprehenditur:* So iemand ein vierfüßig oder ander Thier zur Ungebühr umgebracht, oder ſonſt, auſſer dieſer Fälle ungebührlicher Weiſe Schaden gethan, als ſo einer dem andern etwas verbrandt, zerbrochen, zerriſſen 2c. da mag er der Beſchädigte dieſe Klage L. Aquiliæ anſtellen, und darinnen bitten, daß er, der Thäter, das Viehe bezahle, aufs theuerſte, als es das nächſte Jahr, andere Sachen aber (wenn nemlich einem ſonſten an einem Dinge Schaden geſchehen) als ſolche binnen den nächſten 30. Tagen gelten können 2c. *ex quibus tamen verbis patet, in eo recedi a Jure civili, quod non diſtinguat, an animal quadru-*

E   *pes,*

Regneris, *Censura Belgica, ad* D. 9, 2, 2, pr.; Antonius Matthaeus, *De Criminibus, ad* D. 47, 3, *cap.* 3, § 4; Struvius, *Evolutiones controversiarum. ad* D. 9, 2, § 25; Schneidewinus, *Ad Inst* 4, 3, 13; Brunnemann, *Ad Pandectas, ad* D. 9, 2, 27, 7; Giesebert, *Justinian Harmonicus,* D. 9, 2, 53 where he says that these customs are universal.

§   XLV

Also important are the words of the following § 3 (*Usus Modernus Pandectarum*) which are correctly added to this:

Therefore since the Germans were once content with reparation merely of the damage done, only this one doubt remains with regard to practice, namely whether, after Roman Law had been received, they departed from their original simplicity in estimating damage and received a different method of assessment following the *lex Aquilia*. I would not dare to assert this, since after the reception of Roman Law, the earlier German customs were not utterly abrogated, so that I would think that where it could not be shown that the *lex Aquilia* in this respect was specifically approved, a retrospective evaluation of damage does not take place. However, a place where the specific evaluation of the *lex Aquilia* is approved is shown us by the Electoral Laws of Prussia where in book 6, *tit.* 10, *art.* 1 § 5 it is found provided as follows: "If someone has killed a quadruped or another animal unlawfully, or if he has in any other way unlawfully done damage by burning, breaking or rending, then the person suffering the damage may institute this action of the *lex Aquilia*, by means of which he may ask the wrongdoer to pay the maximum value of the animal within the next year or, if the damage was done to another object, the value within the next thirty days." From these words, however, it is clear that it deviates from the Civil Law in that it does not distinguish whether a four-footed

pes, an bipes læfum ; & an quadrupes gregatim pafcatur vel
non, fed omnia animalia eodem loco babeantur.

§. XLVI.

Et illud addo: Compilatorem Juris Boruffici non
diftinxiffe fecundum difpofitionem Legis Aquiliæ, utrum
quadrupes, quæ gregatim pafcitur, fuerit occifa, vel aliud
damnum ei datum, fed omnia damna animalibus illata in
primum caput Legis Aquiliæ transtuliffe: quod fatis often-
dit, in quantas inconvenientias illi incidere foleant, qui id
agunt, ut e foris Germaniæ Mores Germanorum elimi-
nent, & Jus Civile introducant. Haud dubie Compilator
Juris Boruffici eam intentionem habuit, ut actionem Legis
Aquiliæ invita quamvis Jurisprudentia Germanica introdu-
ceret in Boruffiam *Confer §. ult.* Quantam vero crucem
fixerit Pragmaticis fuis vel ex ignorantia Juris Romani, vel
ex intempeftiva ejus emendatione, vel potius capitis tertii
Legis Aquiliæ cum primo confufione, hactenus dicta fatis
oftendunt.

§. LXVII.

Jam in viam. Cum igitur mores totius fere Germaniæ petant faltem veram damni æftimationem, fponte fluit,
quod actio de damno dato recepta in foris Germaniæ ne-
quaquam fit actio Legis Aquiliæ, quamvis parum apte
communiter Syftematici pariter & Pragmatici loquantur,
dum dicitur, hodie actionem Legis Aquiliæ in foris Germaniæ non dari ad petitionem ejus, quanti res retro plurimi
fuerit, quo nihil inconvenientius dici poterat. Actio fi-
quidem Legis Aquiliæ, quæ non petit, quanti res retro fuerit, non eft Legis Aquiliæ actio, cum in eo conftiterit formalis

or a two-footed beast has been injured and whether or not the four-footed animals graze in herds, but all animals are included in the same text.

§ XLVI

And I add the following: that the compiler of the Prussian Law did not distinguish along the lines of the *lex Aquilia* as to whether a quadruped which grazes in a herd has been killed, or other damage done to it, but he transferred all damage done to animals to the first chapter of the *lex Aquilia*. This shows clearly the enormous inconsistencies into which fall those who do this sort of thing in order to remove German customs from German courts and to introduce the Roman Civil Law. Without doubt the compiler of the Prussian Law had the intention of introducing the action of the *lex Aquilia* into Prussia in spite of the opposition of German Jurisprudence. Compare the final paragraph. What has been said hitherto sufficiently shows what troubles he created for his own practitioners, either because of his ignorance of the Roman Law or because of his unhappy emendation, that is by his confusion of the third chapter of the *lex Aquilia* with the first.

§ XLVII[24]

Now back to business. Since therefore the customs of almost all Germany claim only the true value of the damage, it follows automatically that the action for damage done, as received in the courts of Germany, is in no way the action of the *lex Aquilia*, even although both academics and practitioners generally speak inaccurately when they say that today the action of the *lex Aquilia* is not given in the courts of Germany in order to claim the highest value that the property attained retrospectively. Nothing more inconsistent than this could be said. Obviously, an action of the *lex Aquilia* which does not claim the value of the property retrospectively is not the *action* of the *lex Aquilia*, since in that principle is established the formal

---

[24] Reading *XLVII* for *LXVII* as in the 1703 edition.

malis ratio istius actionis. Fluit etiam ex dictis, quod plane nullus sit Legis Aquiliæ Usus in foris Germaniæ.

§. XLVIII.

Possemus ad alia transire, nisi urgeret Da. SCHILTE-NUS, qui *d. l. th. 59. seq.* In eo totus est, ut ostendat, non nullum plane hodie esse actionis Legis Aquiliæ usum. Age videamus. Ita vero incipit *d. th. 59. Ex hactenus tractatis vidimus, quam una justi ac æqui regula in omnium quidem Gentium legibus cernatur, sed ea tamen in aliis aucta, in aliis minuta, prout legislatori cuique Reipubl. suæ suisque civibus ac eorum moribus commodius aptiusque visum. Liquet etiam, diversam hic in multis esse Legislationem Romanam a Teutonica, ut non immerito dubitari possit, an in foro nostro usus sit aliquis Legis Aquiliæ & inde competentis actionis directæ, aut ejus subsidiariarum utilis & in factum. Certe non male monuit* BRUNNEMANN. ad L 7. n. 11. ad l. 9. n. 1. ad l. 11. n. 14. D. h. t. *differentiam istam actionis directæ, utilis & in factum in foro non attendi: nam in judiciis indistincte eum, qui mortis (cujusvis damni) causam per culpam præbuit, ex L. Aquilia teneri & supervacuum esse adeo (quod in cathedra sit & Scholis) in discrimine actionis L. Aquiliæ directæ & utilis & in factum operam insumere & sollicite distinguere. Recte omnino, quia istæ differentiæ fere ex unici juris Formularii Flaviani apicibus profluxerunt.* Hactenus bene. Nunc vero sequitur, quod emendationem meretur.

§. XLIX.

Ita enim pergit *th.* 60. *Sed nec quod in ipsa directa actione, cæterisque subsidiariis, in petitionem venit, nempe quanti maximi res eo anno vel mense fuerit, id in actione no-*

stri

rationale for that particular action. It follows from what has been said that clearly there is no use of the *lex Aquilia* in the German courts.

§ XLVIII

We would be able to move on to other topics if it were not for the urgings of Schilter who in the said 19, § 59(60) *et seq* is completely involved in showing that today there is clearly some use of the *lex Aquilia*. Come let us see. The said § 59(60) begins as follows:

> From what has been discussed thus far we have seen how one rule of justice and equity is seen in the laws of all peoples but among some it has been increased, among other reduced, as each lawgiver deemed it the more convenient and the more fitting to his state, to his citizens and to their customs. It will also become clear that here Roman lawgiving is in many respects different from German, so that one can rightly doubt whether in our courts the *lex Aquilia* is used at all, and consequently whether the direct action is used or an *actio utilis* and *actio in factum* subsidiary to it. Certainly Brunnemann, *ad Pandectas*, D. 9, 2, 7, n. 11; D. 9, 2, 9, n. 1; D. 9, 2, 11, n. 14, has rightly commented that the distinction between the direct action, the *actio utilis* and the *actio in factum* is not observed in court, for in suits without qualification he who, by his fault, provided the cause of death (or any form of damage) is liable under the *lex Aquilia* and it is superfluous (as happens in Universities and Law schools) to expend effort and punctiliously to distinguish between the direct action of the *lex Aquilia*, the *actio utilis* and the *actio in factum*. Quite correctly so, because those distinctions derive almost entirely from the minutiae of one formula writer, Flavius.
>
> Thus far so good. Now follows what merits emendation.

§ XLIX

For § 60(61) continues as follows:

> But that which comes into the claim in the direct action and in the other subsidiary actions, namely as 'the highest value the property attained in that year or month' is not claimed in the action of our

stri fori petitur, aut a judice pronunciatur, sed ad reparatio-
nem damni tantum agitur, quanti eo tempore res valuit, quo
damnum datum est, & simul ad pænam seu emendam, nisi
dolus juramento purgatus per d. art. 48. lib. 3. & Dd. nostra-
tes.   Quicquid tamen sit, etsi actio de damno culpa dato in
nostro foro frequentata non sit ipsa illa actio L. Aquiliæ, pro-
pterea tamen non est nullus L. Aquiliæ usus in foro nostro di-
cendus, aut actionis Aquiliæ.   Communiter indicium esse
solet, istud: *quicquid tamen sit*, quod rationes dubitandi
sint fortiores, quam rationes decidendi, cum illa formula
nihil fere denotet, quam bene placitum nulla ratione sub-
nixum.   Sed non deest ratio Dn. Schiltero, qua formulam
istam demonstrare satagit.   Quare necesse est, ut & hanc
audiamus.

§. L.

Explicat eam *th. 61. Quæ ut clarius dicam, notandum*
est, quod actio, qua in foro Germanico, & Saxonico imprimis
persequimur damni injuria dati reparationem, participet na-
turam genericam seu communem actionis L. Aquiliæ, quam
hæc ex æquitate naturali & moribus Gentium obtinuit: na-
turam porro propriam Juris Quiritum vix habet, sed suam
sibi propriam, ex cujusque nationis jure ac moribus.   Rem
in summam contrahamus.   Secundum mentem viri cele-
berrimi est aliquis in foris Germaniæ Usus Legis Aquiliæ
aut actionis Aquiliæ, quia natura ejus generica apud Germanos est in usu.   Quid respondebimus? nil aliud, quam
quod a natura generica ad denominationem speciei non valeat consequentia.   Essentia specierum sine differentia spe-
cifica nulla est.   Alias enim sequeretur v gr. Gallinam esse Elephantum, quia natura generica Elephanti, quod animal

court, nor is it pronounced by the judge but a claim is only lodged for reparation of as much damage as the property was worth at the time when the damage was done, and at the same time there is a claim for a penalty amends unless intent has been cleared by a purgatory oath (see the said *art.* 48, *lib.* 3 and our learned commentators). Be this as it may, however, even if the action for damage done through negligence which is very common in our courts is not the actual action of the *lex Aquilia*, there is no reason for our saying that there is no use of the *lex Aquilia* in our courts or of any action adhering to the *lex Aquilia*.

Usually those words *quidquid tamen sit* (be this as it may, however) are an indication that grounds for doubting are stronger than the reasons for deciding, since that formula denotes almost nothing other than that a decision has been made but not resting on any sound reason. But Schilter does not lack a reason with which he is busy proving that statement, and so it is necessary that we hear it.

§ L

§ 60(61) explains it as follows:

In order to speak more clearly, it must be noted that the action with which we chiefly claim reparation for damage done in the German and Saxon courts shares the generic or common nature of the action of the *lex Aquilia*, which the *lex Aquilia* derives from natural equity and the customs of the peoples of the world; of course, our action does not have the special nature of the Civil Law but a nature peculiar to itself, derived from the law and customs of all nations.

There we have the matter in a nutshell. According to the view of this most eminent gentleman, there is in the courts of Germany some use of the *lex Aquilia* or of the action of the *lex Aquilia* because its generic nature is in use among the Germans. What shall we reply? Nothing other than that the inference from a generic nature to the designation of a species is not valid. There is no essence of a species without a specific difference. Otherwise it would follow, for example, that a hen is an elephant because the generic nature of an elephant, i.e. that it is an animal,

mal fit, competit Gallinæ.   Scilicet non confundendæ funt
quæftiones diftinctæ.   Aliud enim eft quærere an Lex A-
quilia habeat ufum moribus noftris, quam recte negavimus
fimpliciter.   Aliud eft: An Leges fub titulo de L. Aquilia
comprehenfæ ufum habeant? Ubi diftinguendum.   Vel
enim illæ repetunt generales doctrinas Juris Gentium, apud
omnes populos, & fic etiam apud Germanos ufum habent;
vel pertinent in fpecie ad Legem Aquiliam qua talem. Et
hæ nullum rurfus ufum habent.

§. LI.

Antequam pergamus ulterius, e re erit difpicere, unde mores hodierni ortum ducunt.   Sane conveniunt quidem cum Jure Germanico medio, i. e. cum fpeculo Suevico & Saxonico in eo, quod & fecundum illud notaverimus,
regulariter actionem de damno competiiffe ad fimplicem
rei reftitutionem.   In eo tamen differt actio hodierni fori
ab actione illa fpeculi Suevici & Saxonici, quod hodierna
femper detur ad rei perfecutionem, illa vero data fuerit
quandoque fimul ad emendam feu poenam Germanicam.
Igitur maxime quær tur, unde hæc mutatio Juris Germanici ortum ducat? Et nulla alia videtur dari poffe conve-
nientior ratio, quam fi dixerimus, eam ortam effe ex Jure
Canonico.   Cum enim fupra monftraverimus, Jus Canonicum in omni damno ex proæref dato, non concedere
privatis læfis actionem poenalem, & præterea initio nota-
ta docuerint, convenire hæc parte Canonicum jus cum æ-
quitate naturali & moribus Gentium, fane in tantum fe
commendavit hac parte Jus Canonicum Germanis ut duritiem morum propriorum ad æquitatem Juris Canonici re-
ducerent: Quo facto plane non fuerunt apti, ut introdu-

also pertains to a hen. Of course, distinct questions must not be confused. For it is one thing to ask whether the *lex Aquilia* is used in our customs, and this we have correctly and simply denied. It is another to ask whether the Laws included under the rubric *'de Lege Aquilia'* are used. Here there must be a distinction. For either those laws reflect the general principles of the *Ius Gentium* and have application among all people and thus also among the Germans, or they pertain specifically to the *lex Aquilia* as such. And the latter, again, have no application.

§ LI

Before we proceed further it will be relevant to see whence today's customs originate. Of course they accord with the law of central Germany, i.e. with the *Schwaben-* and *Sachsenspiegel* in that, as we have noted, the action for damage is regularly available for the simple restitution of the thing. However, the action of our present-day courts differs from the action of the *Schwaben-* and *Sachsenspiegel* in that the present-day action is always given for the reclaiming of the article but the other was sometimes given as amends or as the German penalty at the same time. Hence the very important question "From where did this change in the German Law originate?" And there is no more satisfactory answer than for us to say that it arose from Canon Law. Since we have shown above that Canon Law, in all cases of damage done with forethought, does not grant a penal action to lay persons who have been injured and, moreover, since our initial comments showed that in this respect the Canon Law accords with natural equity and the customs of the Nations, of course, the Canon Law commended itself to the Germans only in that they might bring the harshness of their own customs into line with the equity of the Canon Law. Once this was done, clearly, when the Law of Justinian was introduced

cto, integro seculo post Jus Canonicum, Jure Justinianeo in Academias Germaniæ, relicta hac parte Juris Canonici æquitate, recipere potuerint irregularem illam & omni ratione destitutam duritiem Legis Aquiliæ.

§. LII.

His vero notatis facile intelligitur, quam recte & optime satisfecerit Sichardi invectivæ contra mores hodiernos Dn SCHILTERUS *d. l. tb. 65. Igitur nollem, ait, excidisse JCtorum nostratium maximo, quod ad eandem rubric. num. 13.14. inculcans practicam libelli L. Aquiliæ, ait:* Illis sic præmissis, accedendum est ad practicam, & præsertim ad confectionem libelli in actione L. Aquiliæ. Et cum in omnibus judiciis nulla actio sit frequentior illa, diligenter perpendenda est forma, non quidem talis, quam hodie indocti Advocati usurpant, & indoctiores judices sequuntur, sed quæ stabiliatur legibus & juribus, qualem ego nullam unquam vide in practica. *Bona verba quæso, nec Advocatos, nec judices credo indoctos, qui usum sequuntur fori, quem licet non Leges Romanæ suppeditent, suppeditant tamen patriæ Leges atque Mores ratione civili haud minus destituti. Sed pergit:* Ex quibus jam liquet, quantum erretur hodie in practica: ubi in damnis datis, & in iisdem sarciendis nunquam fit mentio neque præteriti anni, neque tringinta dierum. *Enim vero error haud est, quod Legi alicui Romanæ non est conforme, conforme tamen est, & ipsi Romano veteri, & naturali æquitati & moribus patris.* Adde & Juri Canonico, cujus in Germania quoad jura privatorum semper fuit magna autoritas.

§. LIII.

Simul tamen ea, quæ de origine Morum hodiernorum

rum

into the Universities of Germany, a whole century after the Canon Law, they were not inclined to abandon the equity of the Canon Law in this respect, and receive the irregularity and harshness, devoid of all reason, of the *lex Aquilia*.

§ LII

Once these points are noted, it is easily understood how correctly and elegantly Schilter in the said § 65(66) answered the railing of Sichard against present day customs. He says:

> I would not wish therefore to omit the greatest of our Jurists because under the same rubric *num*. 13 and 14, when emphasising the practice of the written statement of claim of the *lex Aquilia*, Sichard says 'After these prefatory remarks, one must move on to practice and especially to drawing up a written statement of claim for the action of the *lex Aquilia*. And since there is no more frequent action in any court, the *form* must be carefully considered, not indeed such as today's untrained lawyers use, and even more untrained judges apply, but that which is supported by law and legal rights, such as I have never seen in practice.' Fine words indeed, and I do not consider untrained those lawyers and judges who follow the usage of the courts which, although it is not provided by Roman Law, is nevertheless provided by the law of our country and its customs which are no less endowed with a sense of the common weal. But he continues 'It will now be clear from this how much we err today in practice, when in the case of damage done and in the making good thereof mention is never made either of the past year or of the past thirty days.' Now this is not error, because the statement of claim does not conform to some Roman Law; it conforms on the other hand to the law of the early Romans, to natural equity and to our ancestral customs.

Also add the Canon Law, which always had great authority in Germany as far as private law was concerned.

§ LIII

At the same time, however, those remarks which we have made about the origin of today's

rum diximus, oftendunt, quod non bene cohaereant ea,
quae jam fequuntur apud Dn. SCHILTERUM. Ita enim
pergit *th. 66. Denique, ut quod res eft, dicam: Tres funt mo-
di, quibus ex caufa damni injuria dati agi in foro hodierno
poterit, quos nec confundere invicem, nec fi alio prae alio uti
quis voluerit, propterea imperitiae accufandus, quia omnes
funt jure ac moribus probati.* Nos vero non nifi unum
modum agnofcimus, ideo jure probatum, quia moribus
probatus eft, quem videlicet primo loco memorat Dn.
SCHILTER in verbis fequentibus: *Primus atque commu-
niffimus* (nos addimus: & unius) *agendi modus atque juri
naturali ac Gentium proxime accedens, eft, a quo non nifi reparationem damni perfequimur, quae fit reftitutione rei aequi-
valentis aut pretii, five alicujus poenae perfecutione. Haec a-
ctionis fpecies eft moribus Teutonicis tum prifcis tum bodier-
nis tritiffima, & perperam a Sichardo reprebenfa. Nam
quod & Canoniftas* in c. fi bos 3. de injur. *errare dicit, pu-
tantes in libello de bove cornupeta poffe concludi, ut aeque bo-
nus bos mibi detur, ipfe errat, & diverfa remedia confundit.
Receperant & mores Teutonici atque Gothici, & Canones Ec-
clefiaftici boc reparationis genus ex divino Hebraeorum Jure.*
Exod. XXI. Si fciebat, quod bos cornupeta effet, ab he-
ri & nudius tertius, & non cuftodivit eum Dominus fuus,
reddet bovem pro bove, & cadaver integrum accipiet.
*Caeterum bujus actionis ad fimplicem damni reftitutionem
directae formulam, in noftro foro ufitatam exbibet* Dn. SVEN-
DENDÖRFF *de Act. For. c. 3. m. 27. S. 1.* Daß Beklagter den
angegebenen Schaden zuerfeßen ꝛc. *Atque baec neque ex L. A-
quilia, neque poenalis.* Hic initio acceptamus, quod haec
actio neque ex L. Aquilia, neque poenalis fit, & quod adeo

ipfe

customs show that they do not adhere well to that which follows next in Schilter. For he continues thus in § 66(67):

> Finally to explain the position. There are three ways in which one can sue in modern courts for damage done unlawfully. These are not to be confused with each other and if anyone should wish to use one rather than the other he must not on that account be accused of inexperience because all are approved by law and custom.

But we only recognise one method, approved by law because it is approved by custom, namely that which Schilter mentions in the first place in the following words:

> The first and most common (and we add the one and only) method of suing and that approaching most closely to natural law and the *Ius Gentium* is that where we only claim reparation of damages and this is achieved by the restitution of an article of equal value or price without[25] the claiming of any penalty. This form of action is very common in Teutonic custom, both of old and modern, and is utterly censured by Sichard. For he also says that the Canonists in X 5, 36, 3 err when thinking that in a statement of claim involving an ox which is inclined to gore, I can claim so that an equally good ox be given to me. He is wrong and he is confusing two different remedies. For Teutonic and Gothic custom and the church Canons received this kind of reparation from the Divine Law of the Hebrews (Exodus, 21, 35-36), where it reads, 'If its owner knew that the ox was inclined to gore with its horn yesterday and in time past and he did not keep it in, he shall pay an ox for an ox and he shall keep the entire corpse.' But Schwendendörff, *De actione forensi*, 3. 2. 7. 1 ('that the defendant has to mae good the damage specified') shows that the formula of this direct action for simple restitution of damage is used in our court, and that this is not from the *lex Aquilia* nor is it penal.

From the outset, we accept that this action is neither from the *lex Aquilia* nor penal and that

---

[25] Reading *sine* for *sive* as in the 1703 edition.

ipse Dn. Schilterus larvam hanc isti actioni detraxerit. De-
inde cum ipse Dn. Swendendö fferus solam hanc actionem
memoraverit in tractatu suo de actionibus; magnum argu-
mentum accedit nostræ sententiæ, quod formula L. Aquiliæ in praxi plane non sit recepta, partim quod Vir JCtissi-
mus sit praxeos Germanicæ gnarissimus, partim quod nihilominus alias Juris Romani amantissimus, ut vel ex ejus
notis ad ECKOLTUM *l. 40. Pandect.* patet.

§. LIV.

Unde, quod obiter immiscere liceat, merito vapulat
formula illa agendi, quæ in SCHACHERI *Collegio Practico
ad tit. de L. Aquilia* legitur, quam propterea etiam absque
ulteriore nota apponemus, saltem ut appareat, qualem con-
fusionem, etiam in praxi, soleat introducere incautum stu-
dium Juris Justinianei. P. P N saget, daß als N. Augusti,
jüngsthin auf öffentlicher Straffen vor N. Hause fürüber ge-
gangen, N. mit N. bey der Bierzeche in Hader und Streit
gerathen, und einer auf den andern mit Steinen loßgeworf-
fen, Kläger von N. mit einem groffen Steine an Kopff ge-
worffen, und dermaffen beschädiget worden, daß er nicht allein auf Balbier, Medicum und Apothecken, auch sonsten
vermöge beyliegender Specification groffe Unkosten aufwen-
den, sondern auch interim an seiner Nahrung so viel versäu-
men müffen, daß er lieber 200. Reichsthaler entrathen, als
den Abgang an seiner Nahrung erdulten wollen: Wenn denn
in Rechten wohl versehen, daß, wenn einer aus Verwahrlosung, Unverstand, Versehen, und durch seine Schuld, dem
andern an seinem Leibe, Haab und Gütern Schaden zugefü-
get, und um etwas an seinem Vermögen bringet, oder an seiner Nahrung verkürtzet, derselbe nach Gelegenheit der Sachen, dem andern den Schaden, nach dem Werth, als es
binnen

Schilter himself has snatched this mask from the action. Then since Schwendendörff himself has mentioned only this action in his treatise on actions, this affords great support for our view that the formula of the *lex Aquilia* was clearly not received in practice, partly because that Jurist is most knowledgeable of German practice and partly because he was otherwise most attached to the Civil Law as is clear from his notes *ad Eckoltum, Pandects l.* 40.

§ LIV

Hence if I may make some observations *en passant*. That formula for suing which is found in Schacher's *Collegium Practicum* is justifiably criticised. We shall put if before you, however, with no further comment, at least so that it may appear what confusion even in practice is usually introduced by injudicious enthusiasm for the Law of Justinian:

P. P. N. says that when N. Augusti recently walked past the house of N. on a public road, N. got into a row with N. during a beer booze-up, and the one threw stones at the other, the plaintiff was hit on his head by a big stone and injured to such an extent that he had incurred great expenses not only for a surgeon, a doctor and the medicines but also in other respects (details attached), and that in the meantime he had missed so much of his food that he would rather lose 200 Imperial thalers than suffer such loss of food: since it is well established in law that someone who through waywardness or lack of insight inadvertently and through his fault injures the body or property of another, and thus causes pecuniary damage or loss of food, has to make good such damage, as far as injury to property is concerned, according to the value of the property

binnen Jahres Frist, oder Monaths-Zeit gewesen, er-
setzen und erstatten solle; Als fordert Kläger ꝛc. Bittet ꝛc.
daß nicht allein Beklagter der begangenen Mißhandlung und
Verbrechung halber (ob sie gleich aus Unvorsichtigkeit und ohne bösen Vorsatz und Willen geschehen seyn mag) extra ordinem arbitrio judicis billich zu bestraffen; sondern auch Klägern alle Nutzbarkeiten, so er die Zeit über, als er an seiner
Nahrung verhindert, entbehren müssen, und die verderbte
Sachen, was sie innerhalb 30. Tagen am meisten gegol-
ten, neben dem Arzt Lohn, Apothecker und andern Unkosten
in der Cur, auch in Gerichten, und sonsten aufgegangen, (so
hiermit auf 500. Reichsthaler geschätzet werden, mit Erbie-
then, deshalben einen Eyd abzulegen) zu erstatten schuldig
sey.

§. LV.

Sed redeamus ad SCHILTERUM nostrum.   Is ita
pergit *th.67. Præter hanc communiſſimam competit etiam
actio ex Lege Saxonica* lib. 3 art. 48. *pœnalis, cum injuriarum actione cumulata, deferens juramentum reo, quo a dolo
& pœna liberetur.   De hac antea diximus, qua tamen ipsa
in foro minus frequens opinor.* Nos addimus, hanc acto-
nem non solum esse minus frequentem in foro, sed plane
invisibilem, adeoque non poſſe referri in claſſem earum a-
ctionum, quæ jure & moribus approbatæ sunt.   Dum e-
nim hæc actio a temporibus Sichardi ad nostra tempora
usque moribus sit improbata, & non usu tam diuturno esse desierit, pertinet utique ad actiones emortuas.

§. LVI.

Restat tertia.   De hac ita Dn. SCHILTERUS *d. th. 67.*

F   *Deni-*

within the past year or month; therefore the plaintiff claims and asks that the defendant not only be adequately punished on account of the maltreatment and offence (although it may have been committed through carelessness and without evil intent and will) in the extraordinary proceedings according to the discretion of the judge, but that the defendant also be ordered to reimburse the plaintiff for all deprivations suffered whilst he was prevented from taking food, and also for the spoilt property at its maximum value within the last thirty days, apart from the doctor's and pharmacist's remuneration, as well as other expenses made in the course of recovering, in the course of instituting the action and otherwise (which is herewith estimated to be 500 Imperial Thalers, with the offer to swear an oath on that account).

§ LV

But let us return to our friend Schilter. He continues thus in § 67(68):

In addition to this very common action there is also available an action from Saxon Law (book. 3, *art*. 48). It is penal, running concurrently with the *actio iniuriarum*, offering an oath to the defendant, so that he may thereby free himself from intent and the attached penalty. I have spoken of this previously; however, my opinion is that it is not very common in court.

I add that this action is not only not very common in the courts, but it is clearly invisible, and so it cannot be included among those actions which are approved by law and custom. For since this action has been ignored by custom from the time of Sichard to our own day, and has ceased to exist because of such long disuse, it assuredly belongs among defunct actions.

§ LVI

There remains the third way to sue. Schilter writes of this in § 67 (68):

Denique tertio prodita eft ex Lege Aquilia actio pœnalis, &
cum Jure Romano in Imperio Teutonico recepta. Quæ etfi
non ita trita eft in fori ufu, de qua re querebatur Sichardus,
& inde nec Schneidwinus nec Oldendorpius practicam ejus
formulam exhibent: non dubito tamen ejus ufum effe poffe,
fecundum ea fundamenta, quæ in primordio hujus ad Pan-
dectas commentationis jecimus,& quemadmodum Sichardus
ejus formulam commendat. Etenim negamus, quod actio
L. Aquiliæ fit cum Jure Romano in Imperio Teutonico recepta, quamcunque etiam hypothefin de intellectu Recef-
fuum Imperii, de Jure Cæfareo communi loquentium fe-
quaris. Eft enim Jus Romanum faltem receptum ut fubfi-
diarium, i. e. deficientibus actionibus Juris Germanici.
Dum igitur Germani jam habent actionem de damno dato,
quæ plane adverfa eft actioni L. Aquiliæ, & hactenus etiam
nemo in foro actionem L. Aquiliæ ufurpavit,certum eft,eam
cum Jure Romano non effe receptam. Quod vero attinet fundamenta in primordio commentationis ad Pandectas
jacta, ea jam deftruxit Culpifius, ut adeo non opus fit eadem hic prolixe examinare.

§. LVII.

Ulterius vero fequitur ex hactenus dictis, fi actio fo-
renfis hodierna, de damno dato, non eft actio Legis Aquiliæ, fed ea actio, quam Jus Gentium hac parte commendat
& æquitas Canonica; fimul ceffant hodie in foro omnes illæ conclufiones fuperius notatæ in quibus Lex Aquilia re-
ceffit ab æquitate Juris Gentium, Connexio per fe patet.
Antecedens vero hactenus probavimus. Ergo nihil amplius reftat, quam ut ipfas illas conclufiones paulo diftin-
ctius confideremus.

§. LVIII.

In conclusion, thirdly, from the *lex Aquilia* there is a penal action available and it was received into the German Empire together with Roman Law. Although it is not so common in court practice (and of this Sichard complained), and hence neither Schneidewinus nor Oldendorpius provided a practical formula of it, I, however, do not doubt that there can be use thereof, according to those basic principles which we included at the beginning of this commentary on the *Pandects,* and Sichard provides the formula for it.

Now we deny that the action of the *lex Aquilia* was received in the German Empire together with Roman Law irrespective of what theory you follow in interpreting that famous *Recessus Imperii* (of 1495) which speaks about the common Law of the Empire. For Roman Law was only received as a subsidiary law, i.e. where there were no actions in German Law. Therefore while the Germans already have an action for damage done, which is plainly contrary to the action of the *lex Aquilia,* and to date no-one has used the action of the *lex Aquilia* in court, it is clear that it was not received together with the Roman Law. Moreover as far as pertains to the principles laid down at the beginning of his (Schilter's) commentary on the *Pandects,* Kulpis has already demolished them, so there is no need to examine them in detail here.

§ LVII

Further it follows from what has been said hitherto that if the present-day court action for damage done is not the action of the *lex Aquilia* but the action which the *Ius Gentium,* coupled with Canon Law equity, commends in this respect, then today all those consequences noted above where the *lex Aquilia* deviates from the equity of the *Ius Gentium* immediately lapses in court. The conclusion is obvious. We have proved the premises already. Therefore nothing more remains but that we should consider those consequences a little more closely.

§. LVIII.

Potiſſimum huc pertinet tranſitio ad heredes. Jure Gentium actionem de damno dato ad heredes tranſire docuimus *ſ.13.* Actionem Legis Aquiliæ tanquam pœnalem ad heredes non tranſire dictum *ſ.24.* Jure Canonico introductam eſſe iterum æquitatem Juris Gentium notavimus *ſ.23.ſq.* Jure Suevico vel Saxonico ſi res definiri deberet forte multa adhuc diſputari poſſent ob textum in Jure Provinciali ſæculi Suevici *art. 257.* Diebheit, noch Spiel, noch Wucher iſt niemand ſchuldig zu gelten für den andern, oder ob er wieder kein Gericht gethan hat, iſt aber eine Schulde auf ihn gezeuget, ohne die ich ietzo habe genennet, die erzügen Schuld ſollen die Erben büſſen, dem Kläger und dem Richter. Iſt aber keine Schuld auf den todten Mann erzeuget, ſo büſſen das die Erben nicht; Hat er diß Gut verzehret mit den Erben, ſie ſollen es gelten gar. Aber haben ſie das nicht genoſſen, und iſt auf den todten nicht gezeuget, ſie gelten ſeyn nicht. Hic igitur demum regulariter poſt probationem, aut condemnationem actiones pœnales & damni perſecutoriæ, in heredes tranſeunt, & ne quidem poſt probationem actiones de furto, alea, vel uſura. *Vid.* Dn Præsid. *differt. de Uſu act. pœn. in for. Germ. cap.2. ſ.16.* Quid ergo de moribus hodiernis hoc reſpectu dicendum? Reſpondendum, cum actio hodierna de damno dato ſit actio fundata in æquitate Canonica & Jure Gentium: ideo actio hodierna dabitur contra heredes.

§. LIX.

Cum tamen lectores magis reſpicere ſoleant autoritates quam rationes, en aſſenſum David is mevii, JCti

F 2   &

§ LVIII

Chief among these is transmission to an heir. We have shown that in terms of the *Ius Gentium* the action for damage done passes to the heirs (see § 13), and that the action of the *lex Aquilia* as being penal does not transfer to the heirs (see § 24). We have noted that the equity of the *Ius Gentium* was again introduced by the Canon Law (§ 23 *et seq*). If the matter should have to be defined in terms of Suebian or Saxon law, perhaps much could still be disputed because of the text in the Provincial Law of the *Schwabenspiegel, art.* 257:

> On account of theft, gaming and usury nobody is liable on behalf of another, even though judgement may have been rendered against him; but if he has incurred an obligation which I have not mentioned till now, the heirs shall be liable on that account to the plaintiff and the judge. But if no obligation was created by the deceased, the heirs will not be liable. If he has consumed it with the heirs, they must reimburse it completely. But if they have not consumed it, and if there was no obligation in the person of the dead man, they do not have to reimburse.

Thus here indeed the penal actions and the reipersecutory actions for loss only regularly transfer to the heirs after proof or condemnation and not even after proof do actions for theft, gaming or usury transfer. See Thomasius, *Dissertatio de usu actionum poenalium in duplum et in quadruplum in foris Germaniae*, 2. 16. What therefore must be said about present-day customs in this respect? One must reply that since the present-day action for damage done is based on the equity of the Canon Law and on the *Ius Gentium*, therefore the present-day action will be granted against heirs.

§ LIX

Since, however, our readers are more accustomed to look to authorities than to reason, behold the support of David Mevius, a jurist

& juris fcientia, & longa rerum in foro geftarum experientia vere magni. *Hic Part. V. Decif. 39. Actiones ex contractu ad beredes transire tam active quam passive certo jure traditum est. Quoad illas autem, quæ ex delicto difcendunt alia communis juris difpofitio est, non nisi duobus cafibus, fi lis cum defuncto contestata sit, & si ex delicto quid ad eum pervenerit, tenentur. Inde occasio circa actiones disquirendi, qualis sit & unde, an ex delicto, an ex contractu? cum autem id incideret, ubi de damno alteri illato agebatur, inanem esse eam disputationem reputatum est, quod æquum esset, beredem damnum a defuncto ex non observato contractu illatum fine difcrimine, delicto nec ne damnum datum fuerit, quatenus vires patrimonii patiuntur, refarciri, non attento an lis cum defuncto contestata non sit, aut ad beredem ex eo nibil pervenerit. Id confideratum in caufa* GEORG. CHRISTOPH. BEHREN *liberorum contra viduam* JOHANN HORSTMANNS, *die 14. Januarii Anno 1657.* Additque tum in notis: *De Jure Civili etfi aliquis fecus fentire possit, ex æquitate tamen Canonica quæ ad damnum alteri illatum naturalis est obligatio, ad beredes transitoria reddita est, ut teneantur quatenus ex bonis capiunt,* FABER *in §. pœnales Instit. de Perpet. & tempor. action. ubi ait,* eam fententiam ut æquam in foro Luccor. 4. effe fervandam, *ficut in Parlamentis Galliæ fervari docet* PAPON. *in arrest. lib. 24. tit. 11. arrest. 3. & fin. eam præferendam esse ait* COVARRUV. *lib. 3. var. refolut. c. 3.*

§. LX.

Contra DN. SCHILTERUS *in Synopfi Juris privati ad b. t. n. 11. Ex æquitate Canonica beredes bodie obligatos*
esse

of great legal knowledge and indeed much experience of practice in the courts. From his *Decisiones, part. 5, decis. 39* we read:

It has been handed down as received law that actions arising from contracts transfer to heirs both actively and passively. Regarding those which derive from delict, the disposition of the common law is different and the heirs are only liable in two cases, namely if there has been joinder of issue with the deceased, or if the heir has received any benefit from the delict. Hence the need to enquire what the nature of the action is, and from what it arises, delict or contract. Since this used to happen when there was a case about damage inflicted on another, that dispute has been considered pointless, since it is equitable that an heir without distinction should make good damage caused by the deceased because of the non-fulfilment of a contract and also damage caused by delict, but only in as much as the value of the estate permits, not considering whether issue has been joined with the deceased or whether the heir gained anything therefrom. This came up for consideration in the case of the children of George Christopher Behren versus the widow of Johann Horstmann, 14 January, 1657.

Then Mevius added in the notes:

Although someone might feel differently concerning the Civil Law, however, from the equity of Canon Law where there is a natural obligation to make good damage inflicted on another, a transferable action is given against the heirs, so that they are liable up to the amount of the estate. See J. Faber, *ad Inst.* 4, 12, § 8. where he says "in the lay courts of Lucca that opinion as being equitable must be observed." and as Paponius, *Decisiones*, book 24, *tit.* 2, *arrest.* 3, tells us was observed in the Parlements of France and as Covarruvias, *Resolutiones, lib.* 3, *cap.* 3 says must be preferred.

§   LX

On the other hand, Schoepferus[26] in *Synopsis juris privati, ad* D. 9, 2, *not.* 11, says:

---

[26] Not Schilter but Schoepferus as in the 1703 and 1774 editions.

esse vult MEV. *P. 5. Dec. 39. n. ult.* BRUNNEM. *ad d. l. 23. u. 13.* SCHILT. *Ex. 19. th. 37. Jus Roman. tamen in praxi magis est receptum.* BRUNNEM. *ad l. 1. ff. de Privat. delict. n. 6. in fin.* ENGELBR *ad ff. h. th. 10.* CARPZOV. *P. 4. Cap. 12. 9.* Sed non video, cur id, quod Carpzovius cum alio Doctore statuit, magis dici debeat esse in Praxi receptum, quam opinio Mevii & Schilteri. (Nam Brunnemannus Brunnemanno non debet opponi.) Sane uti Schilteri autoritas in foris variorum territoriorum Europæ fundata est, ita & Mevii hodie in judiciis etiam Saxonicis major est autoritas quam Carpzovii. Et jure major est, quia qui contrariam sententiam tenent, adducunt textus de actione Legis Aquiliæ. Vide præter reliquos HARTM PISTOR. *loc. cit. qu. 27.* At actio hodierna non est actio Legis Aquiliæ. Ergo & in hac quæstione, si larva detracta fuerit, sententia Mevii irrefutabilis est. Quodsi tamen ulterius autoritatem desideres, sit unus instar omnium ILLUSTR. ORDINARIUS NOSTER *in Usu modern. ad tit. de L. Aquil. §. 5.*

§. LXI.

Porro Jure Gentium si plures damnum dedissent, unius solutione liberabantur reliqui, *supra §. 14.* Lex Aquilia contrarium statuit *§. 25.* quia hæc actio est pœnalis. Jus Canonicum & Germanicum medium, hac de quæstione nihil. Quid ergo moribus? sufficit, quod mores sequantur Jus Gentium; Ergo larva Legis Aquiliæ actioni hodiernæ detracta, & hæc quæstio dubio caret. Consentit DN. SCHILTERUS *d. l. §. 70. Quando actione ex moribus ad meram damni reparationem, qua pœna culpæ non com-*

prehen-

Mevius, *Decisiones, part.* 5, *decis.* 39, *num.* 4, Brunnemann, *Ad Pandectas*, D. 9. 2. 23. n. 13 and Schilter, *Exercitationes ad Pandectas*, 19, 73 (74)[27] wish heirs to be liable today on the basis of the equity of the Canon Law. However, Roman Law has rather been received in practice. See Brunnemann, *Ad Pandectas*, D. 47, 1, 1, n. 6, *in fin*; Engelbrecht[28], *ad* D. 9, 2, n. 10; Carpzovius, *Jurisprudentia forensis*, 4. 12. 9.

But I do not see why one should say that what Carpzovius and the other learned Gentlemen decided has been received in practice more than the opinion of Mevius and Schilter. (For Brunnemann ought not to be opposed to Brunnemann.) Of course, in as much as Schilter's authority is entrenched in the courts of the various countries of Europe, so today Mevius' authority in the courts of Saxony is greater than that of Carpzovius. And their view is stronger in law because those who hold a contrary view cite texts from the action of the *lex Aquilia*. See in addition to the other Pistoris, *Quaestiones, loc. cit., qu.* 27. Now today's action is not the action of the *lex Aquilia*. Therefore in this question, once the mask has been stripped off, the opinion of Mevius is irrefutable. But if, however, you should desire further authority there is one unparalleled - our illustrious *Ordinarius* (Stryk). See his *Usus Modernus ad* D. 9, 2, § 5.

§ LXI

Further in terms of the *Ius Gentium* if several persons had done damage, and one man pays, the rest were freed from obligation. See above § 14. The *lex Aquilia* laid down the contrary, see § 25, because this action is penal. The Canon Law and the law of central Germany say nothing on this question. What then of custom? It suffices that custom follows the *Ius Gentium*. Therefore with the mask of the *lex Aquilia* stripped from our present day action even this question is not subject to doubt. Schilter agrees (the said § 70(71)):

When we sue in terms of the action based on custom for pure repara-tion of damage when a penalty for negligence is not included

---

[27] All the editions of the *Larva* which I have consulted have Schilt. *Ex.* 19. *th.* 37. This is, however, an incorrect transposition from the original Schoepferus, Schilt. *Ex.* 19. *th.* 73.
[28] Not Excelse but Engelbrecht as in the 1703 and 1774 editions.

prebenditur, agimus, oppido patet, singulos damnum dantes conjunctim non in solidum teneri, cum nulla sit pœna, sed restitutione facta semel ab uno, idem a cæteris pluries peti nequit; veluti si plurium culpa incendium ortum fuerit, damnumque vicino datum & ab uno resarcitum, cæteri liberantur. Etsi vero aliter pronunciandum esse subjungat idem ibidem, si actio pœnalis ex moribus instituta sit, quia tamen hanc actionem pœnalem supra *ſ. 41. 43. & 55.* rejecimus, inde & hæc conclusio corruit.

§ LXII.

Restat illa quæstio, quam supra § 9. tractavimus, quod scilicet Jure Gentium actio de damno dato reparando, detur etiam contra furiosum & infantem, damnum dantes. Etsi vero & hic Lege Aquilia aliter cautum fuerit, quia tamen *ſ. 26. 27.* ostendimus, hujus decisionis nullam aliam rationem dari posse, quam quod actio L Aquiliæ sit pœnalis, hodierna vero actio, larva Legis Aquiliæ ei detracta, talis amplius non sit, igitur & illud necessario sequitur, quod actio hodierna dari debeat adversus furiosum & infantem. Miror equidem, quod Doctores, ubi de moribus hodiernis loquuntur, hanc quæstionem intactam reliquerint, commode tamen illustrationis gratia ad sententiam nostram corroborandam licebit afferre rationem DN SCHILTERI quam habet *d. l. th. 73.* ad decidendam quæstionem de transitu in heredes: *Illa obligationis species, inquit, quæ est ad damni reparationem non personam respicit delinquentis, sed rem ac bona, ex quibus reparatio est facienda; sicut igitur damnum dans obligatus ad damnum resarciendum*

cſt

it is absolutely clear that when a number of individuals do damage, they are not individually liable for the whole, since there is no penalty, but once restitution has been made by one, the plaintiff cannot claim from the others several times, e.g. if, because of the negligence of several persons, a fire arose, and damage was done to a neighbour's property, if the damage is made good by one of those responsible, the others are exonerated.

Now although the same author in the same place adds that the decision would be different if a penal action in terms of custom had been instituted, because we rejected the idea that this action is penal in §§ 41, 43 and 55 above, this conclusion also collapses.

§ LXII

There remains the question which we treated above in § 9, namely that according to the *Ius Gentium* the action for making good damage done is also given against a madman or an infant if they have done damage. Although here too another provision is made by the *lex Aquilia*, but because we showed above in §§ 26 and 27 that no other grounds for this decision can be given than that the action of the *lex Aquilia* was penal, and because the present-day action, stripped of the mask of the *lex Aquilia*, is no longer penal, therefore it also necessarily follows that today's action ought to be given against a madman or an infant. I am indeed surprised that the learned authorities when speaking of present-day customs leave this question untouched. However, for the sake of a convenient example, it will be permitted me to refer for corroboration of my view to Schilter. In the said § 73(74) to decide the question of transferring to heirs he has the following:

That type of obligation which concerns reparation of damage looks not to the person of the offender but to the article or property from which reparation must be made. Therefore in as much as the one doing damage is liable for making good the damage

est ex bonis suis, ita damnum passus habet jus & actionem ad rem ablatam vel corruptam reparandam ex bonis laedentis.

§. LXIII.

Neque tamen plane omittenda est dispectio de pœna inficiationis quam supra ex Lege Aquilia adduximus. *ſ. 30.* Hic vero iterum nobis ocia fecit DN. SCHILTERUS *d. l. th. 46. Caterum quamvis non tantum Jure Romano, sed etiam Salico Francorum inficiationis pœna erat duplum, atque ad id eventualiter in actionis hujus formula semper agi poterat, veluti etiam* OLDEND *petitionem hujus actionis subalternatam institui posse tradit, ſ. 7. b. t.* Usus *tamen fori nostri nec illud observavit, testante & reprehendente* SICHARDO *in Rubr. C. h. t. fin.* Quod vero nove, vere tamen, in libelli fine adjecimus, negantem esse condemnandum ad duplum, id hodie nunquam fit. Est tamen utile. Usque adeo est fortis illa adjectio, ut Judex teneatur secundum illam pronunciare: & nisi faciat, potest ab eo appellari. *Sed quid si nec in appellationis judicio id fit in usu? Certe frustra invehimus in cathedra in usum forensem, quem nec possumus tollere, destituti vel Legislatoria vel Prætoria autoritate, nec forte satis refutare; quum usus fori nostri propterea non sit temerarius aut iniquus, quod non peræque conformis est Juri Romano; quin imo æquitati naturali longe propinquior in multis articulis deprehenditur.*

§. LXIV.

from his own property, so the one suffering the damage has the right and the action for restoring the article removed or spoiled from the property of the offender.

§ LXIII

Nor must we completely omit a discussion of the penalty for those denying liability which we took from the *lex Aquilia* in § 30 above. Here again Schilter provides us with speedy aid in the said § 65[29]:

> But although not only in Roman Law but also in the law of the Salic Franks the penalty for denial was double and in the event one could always sue for same in the formula of this action, e.g. even Oldendorp says *ad* D. 9, 2, 7 that a claim for such could be inserted in addition to the main claim. However, practice in our courts has not observed this, as Sichard notes and laments in the *Rubric* to C. 3, 35 *in fin.*

But today it is never done to add at the end of a petition as a new item, however true, that one denying is to be condemned for double. It is, however, practical. And that addition is so powerful that the judge is liable to pronounce judgement in accordance therewith. And if he does not do so, an appeal can be lodged against him:

> But what if this is not practice in the court of appeal? Certainly it would be futile for us, from our academic chairs, to inveigh against court usage that which we are not able to abolish in the absence of legislative or judicial authority, nor to refute satisfactorily, since the practice of our courts is neither rash nor inequitable, in as much as it does not conform to Roman Law, but rather is found to be in many respects much closer to natural equity.

[29] For § 46 reading § 65.

§. LXIV.

Nec obſtat Sanctio Prutenici juris *l. 6. tit. Artic. 1. ſ. 5.* Es mag auch in dieſer Mißhandlung der zugefügten Schaden der Beklagte, ſo ſich zur That bekennet, einfach, der Leugnende aber wegen der begangenen Lügen, zweyfach vom Richterlichen Amt, ſo darum in ſpecie von Klägern angeruffen und gebeten, geſtrafft werden. Jam enim ſupra notavimus §. 46. Compilatorem hujus juris, etſi ſatis in feliciter, omnibus modis eo allaboraſſe, ut contra con ſuetudinem Germaniæ in Boruſſiam introduceretur actio Legis Aquiliæ.

T A N T V M.

§ LXIV

Nor is there any obstacle in the provision of the Prussian Law, book 6, *art.* 1, § 5:

> The judicial officer, if he is especially requested to do so by the plaintiff, shall, on account of the damage done, punish the defendant once, provided he admits the wrong; but if he denies, he shall incur a double penalty on account of his lies.

For we have already noted in §46 that the compiler of this law laboured in all ways even although with conspicuous lack of success, so that the action of the *lex Aquilia* was introduced into Prussia contrary to the custom of Germany.

THE END

CHRISTIAN THOMASIUS, THE RECEPTION OF ROMAN LAW AND THE HISTORY OF THE *LEX AQUILIA*

REINHARD ZIMMERMANN, REGENSBURG

The text reprinted and translated in the present booklet deserves notice for thre reasons: (i) its author was one of the most influential lawyers of the early moder period; (ii) it illustrates the development of the civilian tradition and it shows ho lawyers started to assess this development critically; and (iii) it is a key text within th history of one of the main branches of the European law of obligations.

I.

Christian Thomasius was the founding father of the Enlightenment in its specifical German version. Thus, he initiated a second German "reformation"[1]. He was philos pher, educator and journalist, but above all he was a lawyer. He was extraordinari successful as an academic teacher[2] and was also a prolific writer. His publicatio (close to 300)[3] cover nearly every area of the law, particularly private law[4], crimin

---

[1] ". . . 'zweiter Reformator' Deutschlands": Erik Wolf, *Große Rechtsdenker der deutschen Geistesgeschich*, 4th ed., 1963, p. 417. Cf. also Roderich von Stintzing, Ernst Landsberg, *Geschichte der Deutsch Rechtswissenschaft*, III/I, 1898, p. 109 who record that his contemporaries placed Thomasius, side by si with Erasmus of Rotterdam, as "praeceptor Germaniae".

[2] On Thomasius' importance as an academic teacher, see Gertrud Schubart-Fikentscher, 'Christi Thomasius: Seine Bedeutung als Hochschullehrer am Beginn der deutschen Aufklärung', *Sitzungsberichte der sächsischen Akademie der Wissenschaften zu Leipzig*, Philologisch-historische Klasse, vo 119/4, 1977.

[3] For a bibliography, see Rolf Lieberwirth, *Christian Thomasius: Sein wissenschaftliches Lebenswer* 1955. The literature on Thomasius is vast. For bibliographies, see Lieberwirth, pp. 157 ff.; Frai Grunert, 'Bibliographie der Thomasius-Literatur 1945–1988', in: Werner Schneiders (ed.), *Christi Thomasius 1655–1728*, 1989, pp. 335 ff.; *idem*, 'Bibliographie der Thomasius-Literatur 1989–1995', i Friedrich Vollhardt (ed.), *Christian Thomasius (1655–1728): Neue Forschungen im Kontext a Frühaufklärung*, 1997, pp. 481 ff.

[4] See, in particular, Klaus Luig, 'Das Privatrecht von Christian Thomasius zwischen Absolutismus u Liberalismus', in: *idem*, *Römisches Recht, Naturrecht, Nationales Recht*, 1998, pp. 233 ff. (first published 1989).

law[5], constitutional law[6], ecclesiastical law[7] and legal theory[8]. He stimulated the study of the indigenous, German legal heritage, although he was also admired as an authority on Roman law. Central, however, to his work was his theory of Natural law, as summarized in his *Fundamenta iuris naturae et gentium* (1705)[9].

Thomasius was born on the New Year's Day of 1655 in Leipzig[10]. Leipzig, situated at a cross-road of trade routes and with an international fair, was one of the commercial centers of central Europe. It was the seat of an old-established and important *Schöffenstuhl* [11] and, since 1409, the seat of one of the oldest German universities[12]. After the Reformation, it had become a stronghold of Lutheran orthodoxy. Christian's father, Jacob Thomasius, was professor of philosophy; he had taught the great Leibniz. At the age of fourteen Christian Thomasius took up his studies at the University of Leipzig where he obtained the degree of *Magister Artium* in 1672. He then carried on studying law, first in Leipzig, later (since 1675) in Frankfurt/Oder. The choice of subject for his further studies had been prompted by his delight in Natural law: his father had introduced him to Hugo Grotius' *De iure belli ac pacis libri tres*, and when in 1672 Samuel Pufendorf's *De iure naturae et gentium libri octo* first appeared, he read it

    [5] See, in particular, Mario A. Cattaneo, *Delitto e pena nel pensiero di Christian Thomasius*, 1976 and the review of this work by Klaus Luig, *Studia Leibnitiana* 12, 1980, pp. 243 ff.

    [6] See, in particular, Klaus Luig, 'Christian Thomasius', in: Michael Stolleis (ed.), *Staatsdenker in der frühen Neuzeit*, 3rd ed., 1995, pp. 227 ff.; Michael Stolleis, *Geschichte des öffentlichen Rechts in Deutschland*, vol. I, 1988, pp. 284 ff.

    [7] See W. Wiebking, *Recht, Reich und Kirche in der Lehre des Christian Thomasius*, Dr. jur.-thesis Tübingen, 1973, pp. 149 ff.; Christoph Link, *Herrschaftsordnung und Bürgerliche Freiheit*, 1979, pp. 253 ff.

    [8] See, above all, the study by Jan Schröder, *Christian Thomasius und die Reform der juristischen Methode*, 1997.

    [9] The title continues, characteristically, . . . *ex sensu communi deducta, in quibus ubique secernentur principia honesti, justi ac decori*. On Thomasius as Natural lawyer see, e.g., Hans Welzel, *Naturrecht und materiale Gerechtigkeit*, 4th ed., 1962, pp. 164 ff.; Hinrich Rüping, *Die Naturrechtslehre des Christian Thomasius und ihre Fortbildung in der Thomasius-Schule*, 1968; Werner Schneiders, *Naturrecht und Liebesethik: Zur Geschichte der praktischen Philosophie im Hinblick auf Christian Thomasius*, 1971; Christoph Bühler, *Die Naturrechtslehre und Christian Thomasius (1655–1728)*, 1991.

    [10] For discussions of Thomasius' life and work in general, see v. Stintzing/Landsberg (n. 1) 71 ff.; Max Fleischmann, 'Christian Thomasius', in: *idem* (ed.), *Christian Thomasius: Leben und Lebenswerk*, 1931, pp. 1 ff.; Wolf (n. 1) 371 ff.; Franz Wieacker, *A History of Private Law in Europe*, translated by Tony Weir, 1995, pp. 251 ff.; Schubart-Fikentscher (n. 2) 5 ff.; Hagen Hof, in: Gerd Kleinheyer, Jan Schröder (eds.), *Deutsche und Europäische Juristen aus neun Jahrhunderten*, 4th ed, 1996, pp. 424 ff.; Klaus Luig, 'Thomasius, Christian', in: Michael Stolleis (ed.), *Juristen: Ein biographisches Lexikon*, 1995; *idem*, 'Thomasius, Christian', in: *Handwörterbuch zur deutschen Rechtsgeschichte*, vol. V, 1998, cols. 186 ff. Of particular interest, concerning specific aspects of Thomasius' biography, his writings and his intellectual environment, are the contributions in the two volumes edited by Schneiders and Vollhardt (n. 3).

    [11] On the nature, and history, of the institution of *Schöffenstühle* (or *Schöppenstühle*: supra-regional decision-making bodies), see Wieacker/Weir (n. 10) 82 f., 135 ff. They managed to survive after the reception of Roman law, "if learned jurists were co-opted early enough. . . . The best example of such a body in an area with both a long legal tradition and a progressive attitude to legal science is the Schöppenstuhl in Leipzig" (Wieacker/Weir 136).

    [12] Only Prague, Vienna, Heidelberg, Cologne and Erfurt could boast older universities.

"voraciously". In 1679, Thomasius took his doctoral degree under Samuel Stryk, one of the central representatives of the *usus modernus pandectarum*[13]. When he returned to Leipzig in the same year, he practised for a short while before he started to give lectures at the local university. His first publications soon followed, among them the *Introductio ad philosophiam aulicam* (1688) and the *Institutiones iurisprudentiae divinae* (1688), expounding his views on Natural law and based on his lectures on Pufendorf.

Both in his lectures and his writings Thomasius pounced upon nearly all the basic methodical tenets of the prevailing (still largely scholastic) orthodoxy. He soon became an "enfant terrible"[14] within the conservative academic environment of Leipzig. His pamphlet *De crimine bigamiae* (1685) further contributed to this reputation since it propounded the view that bigamy is unlawful only in terms of a *lex divina positiva*, not according to Natural law[15]. In 1687 he caused a sensation by announcing (in German) a course of lectures in German: "ein erschröckliches und solange damals die Universität gestanden hat, noch nie erhörtes crimen"[16], as he himself put it. The subject of these lectures was how to imitate the manners and lifestyle of the French[17]. It did as little to endear Thomasius to the Saxonian intellectual establishment as did his pointedly critical and witty contributions to the *Monatsgespräche*[18], a German language journal which he began to publish in 1688 (and on account of which he is regarded as the father of journalism in Germany[19]).

By 1690, Thomasius' position in Leipzig had become untenable. A clash with the

---

[13] Stryk's main work, entitled *Specimen usus moderni pandectarum*, even gave that epoch in European legal history its name. Cf., for instance, Klaus Luig, 'Samuel Stryk (1640–1710) und der "usus modernus pandectarum"', in: *idem, Römisches Recht, Naturrecht, Nationales Recht*, 1998, pp. 91 ff. (first published in 1991). Generally, see Wieacker/Weir (n. 10) 159 ff.; Hof (n. 10) 404 ff.

[14] Schröder (n. 8) 13. Thomasius is described by Wieacker as "restless and disputatious, eloquent, upright and courageous": Wieacker/Weir (n. 10) 251.

[15] On Thomasius' views on marriage and the law of marriage, see Stephan Buchholz, *Recht, Religion und Ehe: Orientierungswandel und gelehrte Kontroversen im Übergang vom 17. zum 18. Jahrhundert*, 1988; *idem*, 'Eherecht bei Christian Thomasius', in: Heinz Mohnhaupt (ed.), *Rechtsgeschichte in den beiden deutschen Staaten*, 1991, pp. 402 ff.

[16] "An appalling crime that had never been heard of in the history of the university": see the reference in Wolf (n. 1) 384. For further details, see Max Fleischmann, 'Christian Thomasius und die akademischen Vorlesungen in deutscher Sprache', *Zeitschrift der Savigny-Stiftung für Rechtsgeschichte (Germanistische Abteilung)* 30 (1909), 315 ff.; *idem* (n. 10) 16 ff.; Michael Maurer, 'Christian Thomasius oder: Vom Wandel des Gelehrtentypus im 18. Jahrhundert', in: Vollhardt (n. 3) 429 ff.

[17] *Christian Thomasius eröffnet der Studirenden Jugend zu Leipzig in einem Discours Welcher Gestalt man denen Frantzosen in gemeinem Leben und Wandel nachahmen solle? ein Collegium über des Gratians Grund-Regul, Vernünfftig, klug und artig zu leben*, printed in 1701.

[18] *Freymüthige Lustige und Ernsthaffte iedoch Vernunfft- und Gesetz-Mäßige Gedancken oder Monats-Gespräche über allerhand fürnehmlich aber Neue Bücher durch alle zwölff Monate des 1688. und 1689. Jahres durchgeführet von Christian Thomas*, Halle, 1690. Cf. Lieberwirth (n. 3) 21 f.; most recently: Herbert Jaumann, 'Bücher und Fragen: Zur Genrespezifik der Monatsgespräche', in: Vollhardt (n. 3) 395 ff.

[19] Cf., e.g., Wolf (n. 1) 387; Hof (n. 10) 424. Generally on Thomasius as journalist, see Hanns Freydank, 'Christian Thomasius der Journalist', in: Fleischmann (n. 10) 345 ff.

court chaplain on the doctrine of god-ordained authority[20], Thomasius' defence of a leading pietist preacher, August Hermann Francke, and a legal opinion in favour of a religiously mixed marriage between a Lutheran Duke and a Reformed Princess[21], alienated the Elector's court, and early in 1690 the Elector issued a rescript which forbade Thomasius to teach and to publish. Moreover, a charge of *crimen laesae maiestatis* was pending against him[22]. In March 1690, Thomasius therefore decided to leave his "fatherland". He went to Berlin where he was esteemed for his "erudition and skilfulness"[23]. Berlin was then the residence of the Electors of Brandenburg whose widely scattered dominions reached from territories close to the Dutch border to East Prussia. Under the rule of Friedrich Wilhelm (1640-1688), the "Great Elector", Brandenburg had become the dominant power in Northern Germany. Friedrich Wilhelm's son who crowned himself King in Prussia (Friedrich I.) in 1701 and who attempted to stimulate the arts and sciences, appointed Thomasius to a position of electoral councillor and sent him to Halle to lecture at the local Knight's academy (*Ritterakademie*). Halle, about 20 miles northwest of Leipzig, had come under Brandenburg rule only ten years previously.

Thomasius soon succeeded in attracting a large number of students, some of whom had followed him from Leipzig. He even managed to entice his old teacher Samuel Stryk away from Frankfurt/Oder. August Hermann Francke, the pietist pastor whom Thomasius had supported in Leipzig, had also moved to Halle and became professor of oriental studies[24]. All of this encouraged the Elector to set up a new university at Halle which should serve as a tolerant, reformed counterpoise to the Lutheran orthodoxy in Leipzig. It was opened in July 1694 and Stryk became its first director. If the university soon established itself as the center of Enlightenment learning in Germany[25], this was largely due to Thomasius. He remained in Halle even when the law faculty in Leipzig, after the Saxonian Elector's conversion to Catholicism, endeavoured to make him return. In 1709 he was appointed Prussian privy councillor and a year later, after Stryk's death, he succeeded him as director of the university. Even in Halle, his life was not free of controversies; when he declared the sharp distinction

---

[20] For details, see Frank Grunert, 'Zur aufgeklärten Kritik am theokratischen Absolutismus: Der Streit zwischen Hector Gottfried Masius und Christian Thomasius über Ursprung und Begründung der summa potestas', in: Vollhardt (n. 3) 51 ff.

[21] *Rechtmäßige Erörterung der Ehe- und Gewissens-Frage, ob zwey Fürstliche Personhen im Römischen Reich, deren eine der Lutherischen, die andere der Reformirten Religion zugethan ist, einander mit guten Gewissen heyrathen können?*, 1689; on which, see Buchholz, in: Mohnhaupt (n. 15) 412 ff.

[22] Luig, in: *Handwörterbuch* (n. 10) cols. 186 f.; *idem*, in: Stolleis (n. 6) 613.

[23] "Erudition und Geschicklichkeit": Fleischmann (n. 10) 35.

[24] Francke (1663-1727) became particularly renowned as an educator and as the founder of the Francke foundations (*Franckesche Stiftungen*), educational institutions which became the centre of pietism. On the relationship between Thomasius and Francke, see August Nebe, 'Thomasius in seinem Verhältnis zu A.H. Francke', in: Fleischmann (n. 10) 383 ff.; Wolf (n. 1) 390 ff.

[25] Cf., e.g., Stolleis (n. 6) 298 ff.

between marriage and concubinage to be exaggerated[26], he was summoned to appear before the Imperial Chancery (*Reichshofrat*). He took his full share of rendering legal opinions[27] that were submitted to the adjudication committee (*Spruchkollegium*) of his faculty[28]. In 1714 he was charged with the task of preparing proposals for comprehensive legislation of private law in Prussia. Thomasius, however, had serious reservations about these plans and so they were dropped, for the time being[29]. As a teacher, he remained inspiring and enormously influential; the most famous among his pupils were Johann Gottlieb Heineccius[30] and Justus Henning Böhmer[31].

Above all, Halle was where the majority of his publications were written. In his treatises and dissertations he remained provocative and continued to fight against intolerance and prejudice. Only in the last ten years of his life does he seem to have lost his punch[32]. On 23 September 1728 he died peacefully; his tombstone can still be seen on the graveyard (*Stadtgottesacker*) in Halle[33]. Throughout his life, he had remained deeply loyal to the Christian religion. The starting point of his philosophy was the Protestant doctrine of the depravity of mankind after the Fall; and the attainment of eternal salvation was the ultimate goal inspiring his thoughts and his actions. He was disturbed by the increasing emancipation of Enlightenment thinking from the notion of man being bound back (*re-ligio*) to God.

[26] *De concubinatu*, 1713; German translation: *Von der Kebs-Ehe*, 1714. See Lieberwirth (n. 3) 107 ff; Buchholz, *Recht* (n. 15) 212 ff.; *idem*, in: Mohnhaupt (n. 15) 420 ff.

[27] See, in particular, the cases related by Thomasius in: *Ernsthaffte aber doch Muntere und Vernünfftige Thomasische Gedancken und Errinnerungen über allerhand außerlesene Juristische Händel*, 4 parts, 1720/1721; for discussion, see Klaus Luig, 'Thomasius als Praktiker auf dem Gebiete des Privatrechts', in: Vollhardt (n. 3) 119 ff.; cf. also Hinrich Rüping, 'Theorie und Praxis bei Christian Thomasius', in: Schneiders (n. 3), 137 ff.

[28] On *Spruchkollegium* (or *Spruchfakultät*) and on the practice of *Aktenversendung* (dispatching the court files to a law-faculty adjudication committee), see Wieacker/Weir (n. 10) 136 f., 139; James Q. Whitman, *The Legacy of Roman Law in the German Romantic Era*, 1990, *passim*.

[29] Wieacker/Weir (n. 10) 261; Wolf (n. 1) 414. Cf. also Rolf Lieberwirth, 'Christian Thomasius und die Gesetzgebung', in: Schneiders (n. 3) 173 ff.; Thomas Kiefer, *Die Aquilische Haftung im "Allgemeinen Landrecht für die Preußischen Staaten" von 1794*, 1989, pp. 94 ff.; Klaus Luig, 'Wissenschaft und Kodifikation des Privatrechts im Zeitalter der Aufklärung in der Sicht des Christian Thomasius', in: *Festschrift für Helmut Coing*, vol. I, 1982, pp. 178 ff.

[30] 1681–1741, Professor in Halle, Franeker, Frankfurt/Oder and Halle, "perhaps the most famous German jurist of the 18th century", author of works on Roman law, Natural law and Germanic private law: see Kleinheyer/Schröder (n. 10) 482 f.; Wieacker/Weir (n. 10) 173 f.; Klaus Luig, 'Heineccius, Johann Gottlieb', in: Stolleis (n. 6) 279.

[31] 1674–1749, famous for his writings in ecclesiastical law and private law; "confidently and happily beavering away at whatever needed to be done–[he] is an excellent example of the practical lawyering of his day": Wieacker/Weir (n. 10) 172; cf. also Hagen Hof, 'Justus Henning Böhmer', in: Kleinheyer/Schröder (n. 10) 74 ff.; Peter Landau, 'Böhmer, Justus Henning', in: Stolleis (n. 6) 93; Wilhelm Rütten, *Das zivilrechtliche Werk Justus Henning Boehmers*, 1982.

[32] See Wolf (n. 1) 415 f.

[33] Thomasius had married in 1680. He was survived by three of his six children. Only one of them, Christian Polycarp (1681-1751) was married with children; see the family tree in Fleischmann (n. 10) after p. 568.

Today, Thomasius is best known for his campaign against witch-hunting[34]. This was triggered by his faculty colleagues objecting to one of his legal opinions and culminated in his dissertation *De crimine magiae* (1701)[35]. Whilst others (like Stryk) had expressed doubts that witchcraft could be proved, he rejected the possibility of the commission of the crime. Witchcraft was – allegedly – based on carnal intercourse with the Devil; but how could anybody have carnal intercourse with a spiritual being like the Devil? A crime which cannot be committed cannot be punished and, as a consequence, all prosecutions against witches should be stopped. The rhetorical vigour with which Thomasius presented his arguments greatly enhanced their impact and contributed to the gradual disappearance of witchcraft trials in the Protestant territories within the Empire[36]. Likewise, Thomasius condemned torture both from the point of view of Christian teaching and as being an instrument of papal domination[37]. None the less, he did not regard the complete abolition of torture as feasible[38].

Thomasius' views on witchcraft and torture (and on many other practical problems, such as the crime of heresy[39]) emanated from his basic methodological and philosophical convictions. These revolved around the central propositions that legal arguments must be based on reason rather than authority and on experience and observation rather than scholastic deduction; that the *ius divinum*, as revealed by God, concerns the individual conscience rather than the polity, whereas the precepts of Natural law, derivable and discernible by human intellect (*ex sensu communi*), whilst also not

---

[34] See, for example, Gerhard Simson, *Einer gegen alle*, 3rd ed., 1973, pp. 9 ff (under the title: 'Christian Thomasius: Der Sieger über den Hexenwahn'); Klaus Adomeit, *Rechts- und Staatsphilosophie*, vol. II: *Rechtsdenker der Neuzeit*, 1995, pp. 58 ff.; Uwe Wesel, *Geschichte des Rechts*, 1997, n. 261.

[35] On which see Lieberwirth (n. 3) 76; Fleischmann (n. 10) 129 ff.; Wolf (n. 1) 395 f.; Manfred Hammes, 'Christian Thomasius: Kurtze Lehr-Sätze von dem Laster der Zauberey', *Juristische Schulung* 1978, 584 ff.; Gerd Schwerhoff, 'Aufgeklärter Traditionalismus: Christian Thomasius zu Hexenprozeß und Folter', *Zeitschrift der Savigny-Stiftung für Rechtsgeschichte (Germanistische Abteilung)* 104 (1987), 247 ff.

[36] See, most recently, the contributions in Sönke Lorenz, Dieter R. Bauer (eds.), *Das Ende der Hexenverfolgung*, 1995.

[37] *De Tortura ex foris Christianorum proscribenda*, 1705; cf. von Stintzing/Landsberg (n. 1) 95 and notes, p. 58. Cf. also *De origine processus inquisitorii*, 1711, and von Stintzing/Landsberg (n. 1) 97 f. and notes 59. For discussion, see Wolfgang Ebner, 'Christian Thomasius und die Abschaffung der Folter', *Ius Commune* 4 (1972), 73 ff.

[38] It has often been assumed that Thomasius' publications paved the way for King Friedrich II's famous decree of 1740 abolishing torture (with the exception of some major offences for which torture was only abolished 14 years later); see, e.g., Rolf Lieberwirth, 'Folter', in: *Handwörterbuch zur deutschen Rechtsgeschichte*, vol. I, 1971, cols. 1149 ff. John Langbein has, however, demonstrated that the abolition of torture was the consequence of a revolution in the law of proof; see John H. Langbein, *Torture and the Law of Proof*, 1977. "The romantic notion that Thomasius' little rehash of the traditional critique of judicial torture inspired Friedrich the Great to issue his abolition decrees . . . is improbable". But see now Mathias Schmoeckel, *Humanität und Staatsraison: Die Abschaffung der Folter in Europa und die Entwicklung des gemeinen Strafprozeß- und Beweisrechts seit dem hohen Mittelalter*, 2000.

[39] *An Haeresis sit crimen?*, 1697; cf. Lieberwirth (n. 3) 60. Heresy, according to Thomasius, is merely an intellectual error, not a wilful offence. Thus, it is not punishable.

enforceable *per se*, provide the parameters for a just legal order; that the only law that is formally binding and enforceable is the one constituted by the ruler for each territory; and that the good ruler has to allow his subjects to enjoy their freedom and their possessions, as long as they do not interfere with the freedom and the possessions of others.

On the level of constitutional theory, Thomasius emphasized the absolute authority of the territorial princes as against the Roman Empire on the one hand, and as against the influence of the Church on the other hand. The Church should have no say in the government of the State (anything else would have been an act of "political popery"). Likewise, the State could not participate in determining the doctrine of the Churches: the secular ruler had to confine himself to preserving the external peace. As far as private law was concerned, the State had to provide a framework within which everybody could enjoy his freedom and the use of his assets without injuring his neighbour. Essentially, therefore, it had the duty to protect freedom and property against infringements, and its governing principle was *alterum non laedere*. The State was based on a radical separation of law and morality. This explains, for instance, Thomasius' opposition to the doctrine of *laesio enormis*[40] and other, similarly patronizing pieces of Roman legislation[41].

After his death, Thomasius' fame was overshadowed, for some time, by the impact of Christian Wolff's comprehensive system of Natural law, deduced *more geometrico* from the highest axioms down to the finest detail[42]. Wolff, too, spent the most fruitful period of his life in Halle; his system provided the basis for several of the Natural law codifications and, in the long run, he became the father of the conceptual jurisprudence which dominated legal scholarship in 19th century Germany[43]. In retrospect, however, Thomasius is regarded as the more original thinker. Friedrich II. (the Great)

[40] Cf., in particular, *De Aequitate Cerebrina Legis Secundae Codicis de Rescindenda Venditione et eius Usu Practico*, 1706. Generally on *laesio enormis* and its history, see Reinhard Zimmermann, *The Law of Obligations: Roman Foundations of the Civilian Tradition*, paperback edition 1996, pp. 259 ff.

[41] See Klaus Luig, 'Der Gerechte Preis in der Rechtstheorie und Rechtspraxis von Christian Thomasius (1655–1728)', in: *Diritto e potere nella storia europea, Atti del quarto Congresso internazionale della Società Italiana di Storia del Diritto*, 1982, pp. 775 ff. and, more generally, *idem* (n. 4) 239 ff. For a different perspective on Thomasius' views concerning *laesio enormis*, cf. Thomas Ahnert, 'Roman Law in Early Enlightenment Germany', *Ius Commune* 24 (1997), 153 ff.

[42] For an overview, and further literature, see Wieacker/Weir (n. 10) 253 ff.; Klaus Luig, 'Die Pflichtenlehre des Privatrechts in der Naturrechtsphilosophie von Christian Wolff', in: *Römisches Recht, Naturrecht, Nationales Recht* (n. 4) 259 ff. (first published in 1991); Marcel Thomann, 'Christian Wolff', in: Stolleis (n. 6) 257 ff.; Tilman Repgen, 'Wolff, Christian', in: Stolleis (n. 6) 656 ff.; Hagen Hof, 'Christian Wolff', in: Kleinheyer/Schröder (n. 10) 446 ff.; Stephan Buchholz, 'Wolff, Christian', in: *Handwörterbuch zur deutschen Rechtsgeschichte*, vol. V, 1998, cols. 1511 ff.; on the academic opposition between Thomasius (and his pupils) and Wolff, see Hans Werner Arndt, 'Erste Angriffe der Thomasianer auf Wolff', in: Schneiders (n. 3) 275 ff. Wolff was expelled from Halle in 1723, since he was accused of atheism.

[43] Wieacker/Weir (n. 10) 255; cf. also the comment by Paul Koschaker, *Europa und das Römische Recht*, 4th ed., 1966, pp. 249.

must have seen it that way. He generally regarded professors as pedantic and "formless" people with whom no educated man could converse. But he excepted from this verdict the "great Leibniz", the last true polymath and founder of the Berlin academy[44], and the "learned Thomasius" who had trained so many of his civil servants in the spirit of Enlightenment[45].

II.

Secondly: what about the significance and application of Roman law in 18th century Germany, and Thomasius' views on these matters? Here we touch upon one of the most complex phenomena within the development of European legal history, which is usually referred to as the "reception"[46]. Since the days of the rediscovery of the Digest and the creation of the Medieval universities in Upper Italy, private law legal doctrine consisted, in the first place, of Roman law and Canon law. Both were very closely related, and both were studied by everyone who went to study law, whether in Italy or at a university in any other country. "Taught law is tough law": in due course, these learned laws were bound to be applied in legal practice. They became the basis of a *ius commune*. The Italian Commentators were the creators of this *ius commune*, but lawyers in the German territories followed suit. After all, they were still living in the Holy "Roman" Empire (of the German nation). Of course, they realized that very often there were city laws, territorial laws and local statutes which, according to the "theory of statutes", enjoyed preference[47]. But this theoretical preference was severely qualified by virtue of the strict control to which these "particular" laws were subjected. They had to be *honesta, rationabilia, nec contra bonos mores* (and what was *rationabilis* was, of

---

[44] On Leibniz as lawyer, see Klaus Luig, 'Die Rolle des deutschen Rechts in Leibniz' Kodifikationsplänen', *Ius Commune* 5 (1975), 56 ff.; *idem*, 'Leibniz als Dogmatiker des Privatrechts', in: *Römisches Recht in der europäischen Tradition, Symposion für Franz Wieacker*, 1985, pp. 213 ff.; *idem*, 'Die Privatrechtsordnung im Rechtssystem von Leibniz', in: Günter Birtsch (ed.), *Grund- und Freiheitsrechte von der ständischen zur spätbürgerlichen Gesellschaft*, 1987, pp. 347 ff.; *idem*, 'Die Wurzeln des aufgeklärten Naturrechts bei Leibniz', in: *Römisches Recht, Naturrecht, Nationales Recht* (n. 4) 213 ff. (first published in 1995); G. Küchenhoff, 'Leibniz, Gottfried Wilhelm', in: *Handwörterbuch zur deutschen Rechtsgeschichte*, vol. II, 1978, cols. 1791 ff.; Gerhard Otte, 'Leibniz und die juristische Methode', *Zeitschrift für Neuere Rechtsgeschichte* 1983, 1 ff.; Hans-Peter Schneider, 'Gottfried Wilhelm Leibniz', in: Stolleis (n. 6) 197 ff.; for further literature, see Kleinheyer/Schröder (n. 10) 493.

[45] The King's remark is recounted by Wolf (n. 1) 417.

[46] The authoritative account, today, is the one by Wieacker/Weir (n. 10) 71 ff., 91 ff. Cf. also Koschaker (n. 43) 124 ff.; H. Kiefner, 'Rezeption (privatrechtlich)', in: *Handwörterbuch zur deutschen Rechtsgeschichte*, vol. IV, 1990, cols. 970 ff.; Helmut Coing, *Europäisches Privatrecht*, vol. I, 1985, pp. 7 ff. For a discussion of how the reception was subsequently evaluated in German legal scholarship, see Peter Bender, *Die Rezeption des römischen Rechts im Urteil der deutschen Rechtswissenschaft*, 1979.

[47] For details, and references to further literature, see Reinhard Zimmermann, 'Statuta sunt stricte interpretanda? Statutes and the Common Law: A Continental Perspective', (1997) 56 *Cambridge Law Journal* 315 ff.

course, normally determined from the point of view of Roman law) and they had to be proved. There was a presumption in favour of the application of Roman law[48].

Thus, in actual court practice, Roman law gained the upper hand. By the end of the 18th century an observer noted that in the area of private law 90 out of 100 law suits were decided according to Roman(-Canon) law[49]. But this Roman law was not the Roman law of antiquity. It was a contemporary application of Roman law which took account of the changed requirements and value systems of the day. The great task of integration and adaptation, begun by Commentators such as Bartolus and Baldus, had been completed. New rules had been created, old rules changed or even abandoned by way of desuetude, rules of indigenous customary law had been incorporated into the body of the learned law aided, not infrequently, by a process of "productive misunderstanding" of the Roman sources[50]. This was the state of private law in Germany when Thomasius started to write. It is usually referred to as *usus modernus pandectarum*[51]. It was, as Wieacker rightly stresses, the longest period in the history of Roman law in early modern and modern Europe and it effected the "fine-tuning" of the received legal doctrine[52].

For a long time, however, there had also been criticism of, and even hostility towards the Roman law, as received in Europe. The first exponents of the new attitude were humanist lawyers like Franciscus Hotomannus[53]. They had emphasized the historical relativity of Justinian's *Corpus Juris Civilis*, they had discovered that the Digest was composed of different layers from various stages of the Roman legal development and that Justinian had distorted many texts, and they had pointed out the differences between the general conditions of life in Rome or Byzantium and in early modern Europe. Thus, they had started to undermine the authority of the Roman texts. In the middle of the 17th century, Hermann Conring had shattered the "Lotharian legend", according to which Roman law had been introduced in Europe by way of a formal imperial enactment[54]. The imperial authority, too, was waning, and with the Holy Roman Empire the prestige of the imperial, Roman law was bound to decline. It no

---

[48] Cf., e.g., Wolfgang Wiegand, 'Zur Herkunft und Ausbreitung der Formel "habere fundatam intentionem"', in: *Festschrift für Hermann Krause*, 1975, pp. 126 ff.; Klaus Luig, 'Universales Recht und partikulares Recht in den "Meditationes ad Pandectas" von Augustin Leyser', in: *Römisches Recht, Naturrecht, Nationales Recht* (n. 4) 109 ff. (first published in 1980).

[49] A.F.J. Thibaut, as quoted by Helmut Coing, *Epochen der Rechtsgeschichte in Deutschland*, 2nd ed., 1971, pp. 77 f.

[50] See, as far as contemporary Roman-Dutch law is concerned, Reinhard Zimmermann, 'Roman-Dutch Jurisprudence and its Contribution to European Private Law', (1992) 66 *Tulane Law Review* 1685 ff.

[51] See Wieacker/Weir (n. 10) 159 ff.; Klaus Luig, 'Usus modernus', in: *Handwörterbuch zur deutschen Rechtsgeschichte*, vol. V, 1998, cols. 628 ff.

[52] Wieacker/Weir (n. 10) 159 f.

[53] Wieacker/Weir (n. 10) 124 f.; Koschaker (n. 43) 105 ff.

[54] Wieacker/Weir (n. 10) 160 ff.; Klaus Luig, 'Conring, das deutsche Recht und die Rechtsgeschichte', in: *Römisches Recht, Naturrecht, Nationales Recht* (n. 4) 319 ff. (first published in 1983); Bernhard Pahlmann, 'Hermann Conring', in: Kleinheyer/Schröder (n. 10) 99 ff.

longer appeared self-evidently right to apply a law that was riddled with contradictions, that had given rise to intricate doctrinal disputes, that was wedded to outdated and impractical *subtilitates* and that had been enacted by despotic rulers of another age and country. Furthermore, the great number and complexity of legal sources contributed to a widespread feeling both of legal uncertainty and inefficiency, as far as the administration of justice was concerned[55]. Thus, if Roman law was not authoritatively binding but had only been *usu receptum*, it was tempting to re-examine whether such *usus* really went as far as had hitherto been maintained.

The crucial question, in this respect, concerned the onus of proof[56]. According to prevailing opinion, a rule of Roman law was applicable unless it could be proved that it was not. Thomasius, on the other hand, maintained[57] that whoever asserted that a rule of Roman law had not been received could hardly be burdened with the onus of proving such an assertion: no-one is required to prove something negative. Or, conversely: the application of Roman law must be proved, as far as each and every individual rule is concerned. In order to discharge this onus, it is not enough to demonstrate that the specific rule in question has merely been referred to but that it has been decisive for the outcome of the dispute. Also, it is not sufficient to adduce a few scattered examples of the application of the rule in order to establish its use in one individual court. All of this, however, only applies to rules of "positive" Roman law. Where Roman law coincides with the rules of Natural law, it is also, of course, applicable in Germany; one might be tempted to say *non quia Romanum sed quia ius (naturale)*[58].

These propositions emboldened Thomasius to examine topic after topic, and rule after rule, in order to determine the application of Roman law in German practice[59]. In some cases, he affirmed its use, though derived not *ex lacunis glossatorum* (from the mud holes of the Glossators) but *ex genuinis fontibus* (from the original sources). In

---

[55] For Thomasius' views on the deficiencies of Roman law, see Bender (n. 46) 39 ff. and the thesis by Wolfgang Ebner, *Kritik des Römischen Rechts bei Christian Thomasius*, Frankfurt/Main, 1971 *passim*, particularly pp. 85 ff.

[56] For what follows, see the discussion by Luig, *Diritto e potere* (n. 41) 784 ff.; and, more generally, *idem*, 'Aufklärung und Privatrechtswissenschaft', in: Notker Hammerstein (ed.), *Universitäten und Aufklärung*, 1996, pp. 159 ff.

[57] Cf., in particular, *Discursus de causis inutilium doctrinarum in Studio Jurisprudentiae*, 1691; *Vindiciae solidae, sed modestae, corollarii: non ita pridem publice propositi, de exiguo usu Pandectarum in foris Germaniae, adversus obiectiones et contumelias programmatis cuiusdam Wittebergensis*, 1692; *De rite formando statu controversiae: an Legum iuris Iustinianei sit frequens an exiguus usus practicus in foris Germaniae*, 1715; *Delineatio historiae iuris civilis*, introduction to: Chr. G. Hoffmann, *Historia Juris Romano-Justinianei*, 1718.

[58] On the origin of this phrase, see Feenstra, (1997) 60 *Tijdschrift voor rechtsgeschiedenis* 531 (in a review of a volume of collected essays by E.J.H. Schrage which has appeared under this title).

[59] See his *Notae ad singulos Institutionum et Pandectarum titulos varias Juris Romani antiquitates imprimis usum eorum hodiernum in foris Germaniae ostendentes in usum Auditorii Thomasiani*, 1713; see v. Stintzing/Landsberg (n. 1) 99 f. Also, a great number of Thomasius' dissertations on individual topics are devoted to this task. For a list of Thomasius' 150 dissertations, see Lieberwirth (n. 3) 147 ff.

many more, however, he rejected it[60]. The present study on the *lex Aquilia* is among those rejecting Roman law.

The overall picture that Thomasius painted was quite different from the one generally accepted: Roman law was applicable only to a very limited extent[61]. There could be no question of a reception *in complexu*. But what did the courts apply in the place of Roman law? Theoretically, of course, the gaps could be filled by Thomasius' rules of Natural law. But being rules of Natural law, they were not enforceable *per se*. They needed legitimation as positive law. Thomasius tried to provide this legitimation by dressing them up as Germanic customary law (*mores Germaniae*). Thus, he stimulated the study of indigenous legal sources which had hitherto hardly received attention in the universities. This was the hour of birth of German (or Germanic) private law as an academic discipline in its own right[62]. It was to see its heyday in the 19th century, under the auspices of Savigny's "Historical School" of jurisprudence[63]. But Thomasius' approach also contained the seed of the controversy between Romanists and Germanists about the true sources of modern German private law: a controversy which overshadowed historical legal scholarship until well into this century[64].

---

[60] For details, see Luig, *Festschrift Coing* (n. 29), pp. 181 ff., with lists of dissertations in which the use of Roman law was affirmed and rejected.

[61] For details, see Klaus Luig, 'Die Anfänge der Wissenschaft vom deutschen Privatrecht', in: *Römisches Recht, Naturrecht, Nationales Recht* (n. 4) 395 ff. (first published in 1967); very briefly also *idem*, in: Hammerstein (n. 56) 166 f. Cf. also Ebner (n. 55) 30 ff. (hardly the twentieth part of the Digest is applied in German practice).

[62] Significantly, Thomasius delivered an independent course of lectures on German private law (*Institutiones juris Germanici*). This example was followed by his pupil Georg Beyer (1665-1714, Professor in Wittenberg; cf. Kleinheyer/Schröder (n. 10) 467). Characteristically, the lawyer most often referred to in the *Larva* (apart, of course, from Samuel Stryk, on whom see n. 13) was Johann Schilter (1632-1705, legal practitioner and professor) who had started to refer to indigenous, German legal rules and sources, though still in the context of his discussion of Roman law. In his preface to the 4th edition of Schilter's *Praxis juris Romani in foro Germanico*, 1713, Thomasius was to state later: "Etenim etsi in hypotesi . . . . a nobis dissentiret, in multis tamen conclusionibus fovet nobiscum unam eandemque sententiam"; cf. Bender (n. 46) 32 f. The "hypothesis", in which Thomasius differed from Schilter (and Stryk) was the doctrine of *fundata intentio*. On Schilter, see Reiner Schulze, 'Schilter, Johann', in: *Handwörterbuch zur deutschen Rechtsgeschichte*, vol. IV, 1990, cols. 1208 ff.; Kleinheyer/Schröder (n. 10) 507. Thomasius' pupil Heineccius (above, n. 30) published the first self-contained treatment on German private law: *Elementa iuris Germanici*, 2 vols., 1735/6. Generally on the origins of scholarship relating to German(ic) private law, see Luig, 'Anfänge' (n. 61) 395 ff.

[63] See, e.g., Wieacker/Weir (n. 10) 319 ff.; Gerhard Dilcher, Bernd-Rüdiger Kern, 'Die juristische Germanistik des 19. Jahrhunderts und die Fachtradition der Deutschen Rechtsgeschichte', *Zeitschrift der Savigny-Stiftung für Rechtsgeschichte (Germanistische Abteilung)* 101 (1984), 1 ff.

[64] See, e.g., Reinhard Zimmermann, 'Heutiges Recht, Römisches Recht und Heutiges Römisches Recht: Die Geschichte einer Emanzipation durch "Auseinanderdenken"', in: Reinhard Zimmermann, Rolf Knütel, Jens Peter Meincke (eds.), *Rechtsgeschichte und Privatrechtsdogmatik*, 2000, pp. 14 ff.

III.

The subject matter of the present dissertation is the law of delict. Ever since the days of Gaius[65] delict has been regarded as one of the two principal branches of the law of obligations. Strictly speaking, however, the Romans had had a law of delicts rather than of delict, for they were not interested in carving out a set of rules and principles governing delictual liability in general[66]. *Damnum iniuria datum* was the one specific delict where they came closest to doing so. It was based on what was undoubtedly the most important statutory enactment on Roman private law subsequent to the XII Tables: the *lex Aquilia*[67]. This was passed in 287 or 286 B.C. and gave the Roman lawyers considerable opportunity to display their interpretative skills. In fact, the provisions of the *lex Aquilia* were extended, adapted, refined and modernized in so many ways that a jurist from the time of its enactment would hardly have recognized the late classical (or Justinianic) delict of *damnum culpa datum* as specifically Aquilian, and any advice based merely on the wording of the *lex* would have been quite inadequate. *Urere frangere rumpere* had been superseded by the all-embracing term *corrumpere*[68]; remedies were granted in cases of indirect causation and even in situations where the substance of the object concerned was not at all affected[69]; fault in the broadest sense of the word became a sufficient basis for liability[70]; the injured party could recover his full *quod interest*[71]; the role of plaintiff was no longer confined to the owner of the object killed or damaged[72]; and the ambit of Aquilian protection had even been extended to damage to freemen[73]. *Lex Aquilia* had become enveloped by thick incrustations of case law and legal doctrine.

This process of extension, adaption, refinement and modernization had been carried on by courts and writers of the *ius commune*: almost imperceptibly at first, with small and hesitating steps, but leading, eventually, to the far-ranging, popular and comprehensive remedy described by Samuel Stryk: "Tituli praesentis usus", he wrote when reaching title 9, 2 of the Digest[74], "amplissimus est, cum omnium damnorum reparatio ex hoc petatur, si modo ulla alterius culpa doceri possit". This transformation was, first

---

[65] Gai. III, 88 ("summa divisio").
[66] See, in general, *Law of Obligations* (n. 40) 902 ff.
[67] For all details, see *Law of Obligations* (n. 40) 953 ff.; Bénédict Winiger, *La responsabilité aquilienne romaine: Damnum iniuria datum*, 1997, pp. 23 ff. and the contributions in Letizia Vacca (ed.), *La responsibilità civile da atto illecito nella prospettiva storico-comparatistica*, 1995, pp. 25 ff.
[68] *Law of Obligations* (n. 40) 983 ff.
[69] *Law of Obligations* (n. 40) 993 ff.
[70] *Law of Obligations* (n. 40) 1004 ff.
[71] *Law of Obligations* (n. 40) 969 ff.
[72] *Law of Obligations* (n. 40) 994 f.
[73] *Law of Obligations* (n. 40) 1014 ff.
[74] *Usus modernus pandectarum*, in: *Opera omnia*, Florentiae, 1837 ff., Lib. IX, Tit. II, § 1.

and foremost, the work of legal practice[75]. Very little of it can be gauged from the writings of Glossators and Commentators[76] (nor, of course, from authors of the subsequent Humanist school). Even many of the writers of the (Dutch and German) *usus modernus* were reluctant to deviate from Roman law. But by their time, the transformation of the *actio legis Aquiliae* was so firmly entrenched in practice, that further doctrinal resistance must have appeared futile. One by one the changes came to be accepted, or at least acknowledged: haltingly and not always consistently but, in the end, the *mores hodierni* triumphed all along the line. And just as the Aquilian delict of the *Corpus Juris* was a far cry from that contemplated by those who had, in the third century B.C., set out to draft the *lex Aquilia*, so it had become manifest, by the end of the 17th century, that the modern law in action no longer reflected the Aquilian delict of the *Corpus Juris*.

One of the peculiar features of the Roman *lex Aquilia* that never appears to have been received in Europe, was the retrospective (or prospective?) assessment of the value of the object killed or damaged, as required by the "quanti [id] in eo anno plurimi fuit" and "quanti ea res erit [fuit?, fuerit?] in diebus triginta proximis" clauses from chapters one and three respectively[77]. Whilst legal writers tried to puzzle out the reasons for these strange provisions, the courts simply assessed the plaintiff's interest "secundum statum praesentem in quo [res] fuit tempore damni dati"[78].

As a result of these assessment clauses, it was possible, in Roman times, for the award to exceed the plaintiff's interest. It was this surplus which in Justinian's view contributed the penal element inherent to the *actio legis Aquiliae*[79]. Apart from that, only litiscrescence could possibly (if somewhat vaguely) be taken to constitute a non-compensatory component of the remedy, justifying its classification as *actio mixta*[80]. Once it had lost these two features, the Aquilian action was bound to change its character. This was widely recognized by the authors of the (later) *usus modernus*.

---

[75] For a comprehensive analysis of the *usus modernus* of the *actio legis Aquiliae*, see Horst Kaufmann, *Rezeption und usus modernus der actio legis Aquiliae*, 1958; cf. also Helmut Coing, *Europäisches Privatrecht*, vol. I, 1985, pp. 509 ff.; Kiefer (n. 29) 58 ff.; Jan Schröder, 'Die zivilrechtliche Haftung für schuldhafte Schadenszufügung im deutschen usus modernus', in: Vacca (n. 67) 144 ff. The following paragraphs are based on my discussion in *Law of Obligations* (n. 40) 1017 ff.

[76] Cf. Rudolf König, *Das allgemeine Schadensersatzrecht im Mittelalter im Anschluß an die lex Aquilia*, 1954; Kiefer (n. 29) 29 ff.; Pietro Cerami, 'La responsabilità extracontrattuale dalla compilazione di Giustiniano ad Ugo Grozio', in: Vacca (n. 67) 103 ff.; cf. also Charles Fried, 'The Lex Aquilia as a Source of Law for Bartolus and Baldus', (1960) 4 *American Journal of Legal History* 142 ff.

[77] Gai. D. 9, 2, 2 pr.; Ulp. D. 9, 2, 27, 5.

[78] Kaufmann (n. 75) 85 ff. The quotation is taken from Stryk (n. 13). On the rule of '*lis infitiando crescit in duplum*' (litiscrescence), see *Law of Obligations* (n. 40) 974, 1019; it, too, had been abandoned; cf., e.g., Christian Friedrich Glück, *Ausführliche Erläuterung der Pandekten*, vol. X, 1808, p. 385.

[79] Inst. IV, 3, 9.

[80] Gai. IV, 9.

"Actio legis Aquiliae hodie non poenalis est, sed rei persecutoria", was the principle enunciated by Simon van Groenewegen[81].

As in a game of dominoes, this change of character entailed further consequences. Where several persons had caused this damage, the injured party had been able, in Roman law, to claim the full amount from all of them[82]. This form of cumulative liability was squarely based upon the penal nature of the *lex Aquilia*. Once, however, it had become a purely reipersecutory remedy, cumulation could no longer be rationalized. "Nam quae ab Ulpiano subjicitur ratio . . . hodie falsa est"[83], and the consequence was: liability of the several deliquents *in solidum*, but if one of them paid, all the others were released from their obligations[84].

Another domino was bound to fall sooner or later: the Roman rule that the Aquilian action was passively intransmissible[85]. Unless legal proceedings against the wrongdoer had already reached the stage of *litis contestatio* (in which case the wrongdoer's death no longer affected the enforceability of his claim)[86], the heir was only liable for any enrichment derived from the delict. It took a surprisingly long time to topple this dogma, for until well into the 17th century even legal practice tended to steer a much more conservative course than in the case of cumulative liability[87]. But in the end it was the *aequitas canonica* that came to prevail, not only *in foro conscientiae*, but also *in foro civili*[88].

Other changes were even more significant, though unrelated to the (reipersecutory or penal) nature of the claim *de damno dato*. As far as the possible objects of Aquilian protection were concerned, Stryk's rather comprehensive formulation ("omnium damnorum reparatio ex hoc petatur") suggests that all limits had come to be abandoned. This was indeed the case. For, firstly, the *lex Aquilia* had been extended, rather surreptitiously, to cover purely patrimonial loss. A small sentence contained in Justinian's Institutes ("[s]ed si non corpore damnum fuerit datum neque corpus laesum fuerit, sed alio modo damnum alicui contigit . . . placuit eum qui obnoxius fuerit in factum actione teneri"[89]) could, if read out of context, indeed be taken to support this extension for it appeared to imply that any form of *damnum* was recoverable, irrespective of whether a specific *res* had in any way been affected or interfered with. "Fundamentum et causa hujus actionis est damnum injuria datum, . . . *quo patrimo-*

---

[81] *De legibus abrogatis et inusitatis in Hollandia vicinisque regionibus*, Amstelaedami, 1669, ad Inst., Lib. IV, Tit. III, § 15.
[82] See *Law of Obligations* (n. 40) 916, 973.
[83] Stryk (n. 13) Lib. IX, Tit. II, § 21.
[84] See Kaufmann (n. 75) 91 ff.
[85] Ulp. D. 9, 2, 23, 8; cf. also Gai. IV, 112.
[86] Cf. Gai. D. 50, 17, 139 pr.; Paul. D. 50, 17, 164; Call. D. 44, 7, 59.
[87] Kaufmann (n. 75) 95 ff.
[88] For the reason why the canonists had always recognized the passive transmissibility of delictual claims, see *Law of Obligations* (n. 40) 1021 f.
[89] Inst. IV, 3, 16 *in fine*.

nium seu res aliena dolo, aut culpa diminuitur" was a 17th century definition of the Aquilian delict[90] which sums up contemporary opinion on the matter. Cases of purely patrimonial loss could arise, for instance, from the bad advice or the unsatisfactory conduct of a case on the part of an advocate but also from other cases "ubi quis damnum dedit sua culpa; sed non in corpus"[91].

Secondly, and no less importantly, since the days of the Glossators, the *lex Aquilia* was taken to cover cases of physical injury inflicted upon freemen[92]. This view could be based on D. 9, 2, 13 pr. and remained uncontroversial. The *killing* of a *liber homo* was a more difficult matter. In the long run, it was the view propounded by the Glossator Azo that prevailed: ". . . tenebitur lege Aquilia qui occidit liberum hominem"[93]. In the course of the 17th century, this became accepted wisdom[94]. But if injury to life led to Aquilian liability, it could hardly be the victim of the crime himself to whom the action was granted. His heirs or relatives might, of course, have incurred expenses for hospitalization, medical care, etc. Some writers confined the availability of the *lex Aquilia* to these and similar items. Others discussed whether the reimbursement of funeral expenses could be claimed[95]. The most important issue was, however, whether the wife and children of the deceased were able to claim compensation for the loss of support resulting from the death of the family breadwinner. It was this claim, for which the Glossators had laid the foundations[96] and which had become a widely accepted addition to the Aquilian repertory by the end of the 17th century[97].

About the only requirement of Aquilian liability that remained essentially unchanged was *culpa* (in the sense of fault). This could take the form of intention (*dolus*) or negligence (*culpa* in the narrow sense, as it was conceptualized in the

[90] Georg Adam Struve, *Syntagma jurisprudentiae secundum ordinem Pandectarum concinnatum*, Jena, 1702, Exerc. XIV, Lib. IX, Tit. II, XX; cf. also Wolfgang Adam Lauterbach, *Collegium theoretico-practicum*, Tubingae, 1723 ff., Lib. IX, Tit. II, VII ("Ut damnum sit datum pecuniarium, scilicet, quo alterius diminuitur patrimonium").
[91] Lauterbach (n. 90) Lib. IX, Tit. II, XV; cf. also Schröder (n. 74) 144 ff. For Roman-Dutch law, see Wolfgang Freiherr Raitz von Frentz, *Lex Aquilia und Negligence: Der Schutz des Vermögens im südafrikanischen Deliktsrecht*, 2000.
[92] On the development of the claim for compensation for pain, suffering and disfigurement (rooted in Germanic customary law), see Robert Feenstra, 'Théories sur la responsabilité civile en cas d'homicide et en cas de lésion corporelle avant Grotius', in: *idem*, *Fata iuris romani*, 1974, S. 327 ff. (first published in 1959); *idem*, 'Réparation du dommage et prix de la douleur chez les auteurs du droit savant, du droit naturel et du droit romano-hollandais', in: Bernard Durand, Jean Poirier, Jean-Pierre Royer (eds.), *La douleur et le droit*, 1997, pp. 411 ff.; *Law of Obligations* (n. 40) 1026 f.
[93] Azo, *Summa Codicis*, Lugduni, 1552, Lib. III, *De lege Aquilia* (p. 89, left column). For a detailed analysis, see Robert Feenstra, 'Die Glossatoren und die actio legis Aquiliae utilis bei Tötung eines freien Menschen', in: Eltjo J.H. Schrage, *Das römische Recht im Mittelalter*, 1987, pp. 205 ff.
[94] For details, see Kaufmann (n. 75) 34 ff., 43 ff.
[95] See the references in *Law of Obligations* (n. 40) 1025.
[96] Feenstra (n. 93) 205 ff.
[97] Cf., e.g., Johannes Voet, *Commentarius ad Pandectas*, Parisiis, 1827/9, Lib. IX, Tit. II, XI; cf. also Struve (n. 90) Exerc. XIV, Lib. IX, Tit. II, XXII; Glück (n. 78) 341 ff.

Justinianic sources). Wrongfulness remained an essential prerequisite for delictual liability, but was not terminologically distinguished from fault[98]. A general theory of causation was never developed or applied[99]. The difference between *causam mortis dare* and *occidere*[100] continued to be discussed, although it had lost all significance. What mattered was whether the wrongdoer had provided *occasionem damni*, but that inquiry was often linked up with the broader problem of fault.

All in all, I think one can understand, perhaps even sympathize with, Christian Thomasius' emphatic rejection of any link between the Roman *lex Aquilia* and the modern delict *de damno dato*. His treatise was designed to put an end to the kind of mummery that was going on. Let us tear away the Aquilian mask and let us face the modern legal reality, he said: it is time, at long last, to rid the discussion of its Roman encumbrances and to reconsider the fundamental issues of delictual liability on a rational basis. Historically, as we would see it today, Thomasius was wrong. But in terms of legal doctrine, he had a valid point. Though the enactment from the third century B.C. was still (in the words of Wolfgang Adam Lauterbach) "causa efficiens remota ex quo oritur actio"[101], many new strands had been woven into it. The *usus modernus* of the Aquilian delict had absorbed Germanic customary law, some elements from Canon law and medieval moral theology, but above all it had been shaped by the efforts of generations of judges and counsel: practical lawyers who made the *lex Aquilia* suit the needs of their time. Thus, it was part and parcel of a vigorous, yet flexible *jurisprudentia forensis*. But the time was clearly ripe for a new theoretical framework. Contemporary *tractatus, discursus, collegia* and *commentarii* were still full of doctrinal ballast: distinctions between *actiones in factum, utiles* and *directae*, between *occidere* and *causam mortis praebere*, or between the computation of the *interesse* in chapter one and that prescribed in chapter three, litiscrescence and the problem of the penal nature or otherwise of the action, the requirement of *corruptio rei* and the principle of *liberum corpus nullam recipit aestimationem*: all this was more or less respectfully dragged along even though it had become increasingly redundant in view of the *mores hodiernae*. Reference to the latter was all too often merely added, fairly abruptly, at the end of the respective section of the treatise. Legal theory had failed to provide a suitable doctrinal edifice to accommodate the law in action. This task was finally undertaken by the Natural lawyers, and it was in fact the vitality of their ideas that inspired Thomasius to strip off the Aquilian mask.

The new foundations had been laid by Hugo Grotius about eighty years before the publication of Thomasius' *Larva*. According to Grotius an obligation could arise from three sources: *pactio, maleficium* and *lex. Maleficium* was his word for delict, and he

---

[98] See Kaufmann (n. 75) 73 ff.
[99] See Kaufmann (n. 75) 64 ff.
[100] Dieter Nörr, *Causa mortis*, 1986; *Law of Obligations* (n. 40) 976 ff.
[101] Lauterbach (n. 90), Lib. IX, Tit. II, III and II.

defined it in terms that have become famous: "Maleficium hic appellamus culpam omnem, sive in faciendo, sive in non faciendo, pugnantem cum eo quod aut homines communiter, aut pro ratione certae qualitatis facere debent. Ex tali culpa obligatio naturaliter oritur, si damnum datum est, nempe ut id resarciatur"[102]. This was the principal and fundamental proposition of the "Natural" law of delict: if someone causes damage because he does what he ought not to do, he is obliged to make it good[103]. Samuel Pufendorf elaborated the moral foundations of this principle. Innate in man is what he calls *socialitas*: he has to live, and get on, with his fellow human beings[104]. The most important precept flowing from man's social nature is this: "(I.) Ut ne quis alterum laedat, utque (II.) si quod damnum alteri dederit, id reparet"[105]. (I.), incidentally, is the second of Ulpian's three fundamental *iuris praecepta*: "honeste vivere, alterum non laedere, suum cuique tribuere"[106]. It is based, ultimately, on the golden rule of moral philosophy: "Do as you would be done by" – a point, perhaps most clearly emphasized by Christian Thomasius in the present dissertation.

This dissertation was not the first place where Thomasius sketched the basic princi-ples of the law of delict, *iure naturali*. In the *Institutiones Jurisprudentiae Divinae* (1688) he had already emphasized the fundamental rule of *neminem laede*. Protection extends both to *bona corporis* and *bona fortunae* (*divitiae*). The damage must be made good ("damnum datum resarci") no matter whether it was caused directly or indirectly, intentionally or negligently, by commission or omission[107]. The discussion in *Larva legis Aquiliae* resumes the theme. But here it receives its specific thrust from the polemical confrontation with the Roman *actio legis Aquiliae*. Thomasius sets out to demonstrate (i) that the latter is entirely different from the principles of Natural law; (ii) that the action for damage done, as applied in contemporary practice, is in confor-

---

[102] Hugo Grotius, *De jure belli ac pacis libri tres*, Amsterdami, 1631, Lib. II, Cap. XVII, I. Cf. also *idem, Inleiding tot de Hollandsche Rechtsgeleertheyd*, ed. and tr. by Robert Warden Lee, 2nd ed., 1953, III XXXII, 3-6, 7, 9, 12, 20 (referring not only to the *burgher-wet* (positive law) but also to *het aengheboren recht* (law of nature) and stating that the former in this matter adheres more closely to the latter).

[103] For a discussion, see Hans-Peter Benöhr, 'Außervertragliche Schadensersatzpflicht ohne Verschulden? Die Argumente der Naturrechtslehren und -kodifikationen', *Zeitschrift der Savigny-Stiftung für Rechtsgeschichte (Romanistische Abteilung)* 93 (1976), 209 ff.; Kiefer (n. 29) 78 ff.; Robert Feenstra, 'Das Deliktsrecht bei Grotius, insbesondere der Schadensersatz bei Tötung und Körperverletzung', in: Robert Feenstra, Reinhard Zimmermann (eds.), *Das römisch-holländische Recht: Fortschritte des Zivilrechts im 17. und 18. Jahrhundert*, 1992, pp. 429 ff. Feenstra (p. 430) draws attention to the fact that *culpa* in Grotius' formula is difficult to translate; it vacillates between the wrongful act as such and negligence.

[104] Cf., e.g., Samuel Pufendorf, *De jure naturae et gentium libri octo*, Francofurti ad Moenum, 1694, Lib. II, Cap. III, XV.

[105] *De jure naturae et gentium* (n. 104), Lib. III, Cap. I, I; cf. further Benöhr (n. 103) 213 ff.; Kiefer (n. 29) 83 ff.

[106] D. 1, 1, 10, 1.

[107] *Institutiones*, Lib. II, Tit. V, 6, 11, 20, 21 and 34. On Thomasius' views concerning delictual liability, see Kiefer (n. 29) 87 ff.; Berthold Kupisch, 'La responsabilità da atto illecito nel diritto naturale', in: Vacca (n. 67) 138 ff. On the relationship between delict and quasi-delict, according to Thomasius, see Reiner Hochstein, *Obligationes quasi ex delicto*, 1971, pp. 109 ff.

mity with the principles of Natural law; and that therefore (iii) the *actio legis Aquiliae* has not been received in Germany. Thus, the *Larva* is divided, roughly, into three parts: I-XV: the law of delict according to the principles of Natural law: XVI-XXX: in which ways the *actio legis Aquiliae* differs from the principles of Natural law; XXXI-LXIV: the action for damage done in contemporary practice – its history, its conformity with the principles of Natural law and its rejection of the *lex Aquilia*[108]. As in many other cases, Thomasius managed, under cover of contemporary practice (*mores Germaniae*), to turn his principles of Natural law into *ius positivum*.

Much of the discussion in the *Larva* is, of course, of historical significance only. The booklet contributed to the establishment of a modern and critical approach towards the law of delict. It appeared at a crucial juncture, for it integrated for the first time, in this area of the law, contemporary practice (*usus modernus*) and Natural law theory. It drew attention to sources, other than Roman law, that have shaped the civilian tradition. And it pointed out the contingency, in historical perspective, of the rules of Roman law. But there are also a number of passages which should still appeal to modern lawyers interested in the doctrinal foundations of the law of delict. Why, to mention the most interesting example, should the obligation to make good damage arise only in case of fault[109]? This is by no means as self-evident (or "natural") as the assertions by all those who were inspired by Grotius' magisterial formula[110] make it sound. If the basic precept is *alterum non laedere*, *strict* liability based merely on the fact that one person caused the other damage may well be seen to be the more appropriate consequence. This was, in fact, the point of view adopted by Thomasius. "Aequum non solum, sed et justum est, ut damnum casu datum resarciam", he postulated[111] and

---

[108] Interestingly, Thomasius devotes considerable space (XXXI-XXXVII) to elaborating on the significant contribution of Canon law towards more rational rules of delictual liability. This is remarkable in view of his general hostility towards all emanations, and instruments, of papal rule; see, e.g., Bender (n. 46) 41. In XXXVI of the *Larva*, Thomasius specifically refers to "aequitas Juris Canonici".

[109] As was pointed out above (n. 103), the use of the term *culpa* in Grotius' *De jure belli ac pacis* is not entirely clear. At any rate, it becomes clear from his discussion both in *De jure belli ac pacis* and in his *Inleiding*, that he accepted instances of strict liability only as far as the *ius positivum*, not as far as the *ius naturale* was concerned: see *Inleiding* (n. 102) III, XXXII, 22 read in conjunction with III, XXXVIII (*misdaed door wetduiding* = wrongs by construction of law (tr. Lee), i.e. the *obligationes quasi ex maleficio* of Inst. III, 13, 2); *De jure belli ac pacis* (n. 102) Lib. II, Cap. XVII, XX f. The matter is discussed and further explored in an article by Robert Feenstra, 'Grotius' doctrine of liability for negligence: its origin and its influence in Civil Law countries until modern codifications', due to appear in a forthcoming volume of the Comparative Studies in Continental and Anglo-American Legal History under the title 'Negligence' and edited by E.J.H. Schrage. Feenstra states, in the conclusion of his article, that Grotius' concept of "wrongs by construction of law", as a civil law correction of the natural fault-principle, "elicited practically no response, even in his own country".

[110] For all details, see the article by Robert Feenstra referred to in the previous note.

[111] *Larva legis Aquiliae*, § IV. This proposition is related to the fact that, according to Thomasius, the obligation to make good damage done is based on equity and flows from the concept of ownership (see *Larva* X); this is also emphasized by Kupisch (n. 107) 141. Thus, it can be compared to the *rei vindicatio*. Thomasius reconciles the *ius gentium* (liability based merely on causation of the damage) and the positive

provided the example of the crystal glass which is dropped by a visiting friend. Indeed, there is much to be said for making the friend liable, for he is "closer" to the loss than the owner who would otherwise have to carry it (*casum sentit dominus*)[112]. After all, the law of delict does not impose penalties for morally blameworthy conduct but is aimed at achieving the fair distribution of a loss that has occurred.

Thomasius' view did not prevail, and both among the later Natural lawyers and in 19th century pandectist scholarship the principle that liability is based on fault acquired the status of an unquestionable, axiomatic truth[113]: with the result that the notion of strict liability was (almost) entirely removed from the province of the law of delict. Today, however, we have started to question the soundness of this conceptual frame-work. New instances of strict liability, imposed by special statute, are no longer kept isolated from the mainstream of private-law legal theory and attempts have been made to formulate general rules and criteria in order to devise a two-track system of extra-contractual liability[114]. Moreover, it has been realized that in a variety of cases a stricter-than-normal form of liability has grown up surreptitiously and has tended to undermine the borderline between fault- and risk-based liability[115]. Does no-fault liability, therefore, merely represent the bottom line on a sliding scale of liability law? Does not the very notion of an "objective" standard of negligence (*Fahrlässigkeit*) under-mine the foundation of a fault-based liability[116]? What is the practical relevance of "fault" if the crucial policy-decisions are made s.v. unlawfulness (*Rechtswidrigkeit*)[117]?

---

law (which requires fault) by taking recourse to a change of onus of proof; see *Larva* VIII and Kupisch (n. 107) 141.

[112] Blackburn, J., in the famous case of *Rylands v. Fletcher* [1861-73] All E.R. 1, at 11 appears to have had something similar in mind, for his way of arguing implies that he regarded no-fault liability as the primary principle of delictual liability, negligence as an exception (cf. also A.W.B. Simpson, 'Legal Liability for Bursting Reservoirs: The Historical Context of Rylands v. Fletcher', (1984) 13 *Journal of Legal Studies* 213 ff.). In the course of the 19th century, English courts vacillated on the question whether to deduce negligence-based liability or no-fault liability from the maxim of *sic utere tuo ut alienum non laedas*.

[113] For details, see *Law of Obligations* (n. 40) 1033 ff.; for England, see *Law of Obligations* (n. 40) 1138 ff., for Scotland, see the contributions by Reinhard Zimmermann and Philip Simpson on 'Strict Liability' and 'Liability among Neighbours', in: Reinhard Zimmermann, Kenneth Reid (eds.), *A History of Private Law in Scotland*, vol. II, *Obligations*, in preparation.

[114] Cf., as far as Germany is concerned, for example, Michael R. Will, *Quellen erhöhter Gefahr*, 1980, and Hein Kötz, 'Gefährdungshaftung', in: *Gutachten und Vorschläge zur Überarbeitung des Schuldrechts*, vol. II, 1981, pp. 1786 ff. For a justification of both fault-based and strict liability, see James Gordley, 'Tort Law in the Aristotelian Tradition', in: David G. Owen (ed.), *Philosophical Foundations of Tort Law*, paperback edition 1997, pp. 130 ff., 151 ff.

[115] Cf. the discussion and the references in *Law of Obligations* (n. 40) 1132 f., 1140 f.

[116] For a recent discussion, see Helmut Koziol, 'Liability Based on Fault: Subjective or Objective Yardstick?', (1998) 5 *Maastricht Journal of European and Comparative Law* 111 ff.

[117] For a particularly lucid exposition of how "wrongfulness" emerged as a central criterion for delictual liability in Roman-Dutch law in South Africa, see Dale Hutchison, 'Delictual Liability II', in: Reinhard Zimmermann, Daniel Visser (eds.), *Southern Cross: Civil Law and Common Law in South Africa*, 1996, pp. 595 ff. For Germany, see Ernst von Caemmerer, Wandlungen des Deliktsrechts, in: *idem*, *Gesammelte Schriften*, vol. I, 1968, pp. 478 ff.

Essentially, the question of the proper criteria for "imputing" a loss to a particular person is still, or rather, is once again, open[118]. It is worth noting, in this context, that Thomasius stressed the original definition of the delict in Roman law (*damnum iniuria datum* rather than *damnum culpa datum*)[119], and that he advocated the liability of madmen and infants[120]. *Iniuria* (unlawfulness), Jan Schröder has demonstrated, became the all-important tool for limiting a liability which, *iure naturae*, covered every loss, including purely patrimonial loss[121]. Madmen and infants were made liable for damage done by the great Natural law codifications in Prussia and Austria[122]. The respective rules, of course, do not tally with the fault-principle; they are based on "natural equity". It is quite remarkable that a number of more modern codifications have, none the less, followed suit[123].

It remains to be mentioned that, in the days of Thomasius, dissertations were written by the professor rather than the doctoral candidate[124]. The latter merely had to defend the propositions contained in the dissertation in a public disputation in front of the faculty. There is no reason to think that the matter would have been different in the present case[125]. The doctoral candidate was Gaius Matthias Arend from Wismar[126], but we must presume that his dissertation was written by Thomasius himself. The disputation took place on 28 April 1703. *Larva legis Aquiliae* appeared in print in 1703; it was reprinted, in the form of a *tractatio iuridica* under Thomasius' name only in 1703, 1743, 1750 and 1774[127]. We have used here the edition of 1750 which appeared in Halle[128].

---

[118] See, for instance, the contributions in David G. Owen, *Philosophical Foundations of Tort Law*, paperback edition 1997.

[119] For a discussion of the shift in Roman jurisprudence from *damnum iniuria datum* to *damnum culpa datum*, see *Law of Obligations* (n. 40) 998 ff.

[120] *Larva legis Aquiliae*, § LXII.

[121] Schröder (n. 75) 149 ff. The position is very similar in modern Roman-Dutch law in South Africa; here, too, extracontractual liability for pure economic loss is recognized in principle (the leading case is *Administrateur, Natal v. Trust Bank van Afrika Bpk.*, 1979 (3) SA 824 (A)) whereas wrongfulness is the decisive criterion for preventing run-away-liability (of crucial importance was *Minister van Polisie v. Ewels*, 1975 (3) SA 590 (A)). For details, see Hutchison (n. 117) 624 ff. and Raitz-Frentz (n. 91) § 6.

[122] §§ 41–44 I 6 PrALR and § 1310 ABGB.

[123] For a comprehensive comparative discussion of the problem (which he considers to be, in spite of its limited practical relevance, an extraordinarily attractive object of study), see Christian von Bar, *Gemeineuropäisches Deliktsrecht*, vol. I, 1996, nn. 75 ff.

[124] See, for example, the discussion by Schubart-Fikentscher (n. 2) 33 ff.

[125] Even the dissertation on torture, referred to in n. 37, is not really an exception from this rule; Stintzing/Landsberg (n. 1) notes 58 refer to a *Kunstgriff* (artifice).

[126] On whom see Filippo Ranieri, *Biographisches Repertorium der Juristen im Alten Reich, 16.-18. Jahrhundert*, 1989, p. 180.

[127] See Ranieri (n. 126) 323; cf. also Lieberwirth (n. 3) 82 who, however, does not mention the editions of 1703 and 1774.

[128] The 1750 edition is better suited for the purposes of reproduction than the one printed in 1774. Margaret Hewett has compared it with the first edition in 1703 and with the 1774 edition and has marked differences in the footnotes to the English translation.

Lightning Source UK Ltd.
Milton Keynes UK
UKHW022311130622
404351UK00005B/912